About the Authors

Larry Ainsworth and **Jan Christinson**, co-authors of *Student Generated Rubrics: An Assessment Model to Help All Students Succeed*, (Dale Seymour Publications, New York, 1998) have trained teachers, subject-matter coordinators, curriculum directors, and administrators across the United States in performance-based assessment and mathematics.

Larry is a senior consultant and senior vice-president of the Center for Performance Assessment in Denver, Colorado. He travels widely throughout the United States to assist school districts in implementing standards and standards-based performance assessments in the K-12 classroom. He also conducts seminars in data-driven decision making, as well as workshops based on *Student Generated Rubrics* and *Five Easy Steps to a Balanced Math Program*. In 2000 Larry conducted standards-based performance assessment training for the California International Studies Project in conjunction with Stanford University and presented workshops for the National School Conference Institute and for the national ASCD Annual Conference. With 24 years experience as an upper elementary and middle school classroom teacher in demographically diverse schools, Larry holds a master's degree in educational administration.

Jan has 25 years of teaching experience in primary, intermediate, and middle school grades and currently teaches seventh grade mathematics. He also instructs beginning teachers in MSAT test preparation classes at several California State universities. Jan is past co-chair of his district's K-12 math committee, a multiple-term district math mentor, and co-author of the CAMP-LA calculator materials. He served Carlsbad Unified School District in Carlsbad, California, as summer school principal for two years. Jan holds a master's degree in reading and a preliminary California administrative credential.

Five *Easy Steps*

Balanced
Math Program

A Practical Guide for K-8 Classroom Teachers

Larry
Ainsworth

Jan
Christinson

Advanced Learning Press
Denver, Colorado

ISBN #0-9644955-5-4

Five Easy Steps to a Balanced Math Program by Larry Ainsworth and Jan Christinson
Edited by Allison W. Schumacher

Printed and Bound in the United States of America

Published by Advanced Learning Press

Distributed by:

Center for Performance Assessment

317 Inverness Way South • Suite 150 • Englewood, CO 80112
(303) 504-9312 • (800) 844-6599 • Fax: (303) 504-9417
Web Site: www.makingstandardswork.com

Quantity Discounts:

Advanced Learning Press books are available for quantity discounts with bulk purchases for education systems, professional orgganizations, or sales promotion use. For more details and discount information, contact Advanced Learning Press at (800) 844-6599 or fax (303) 504-9417.

Library of Congress Control Number: 00-133985

Acknowledgments

Larry would first like to thank his wife, Candace, for her continuous love, loyalty, and support. He also wishes to extend sincere thanks to Dr. Douglas Reeves of the Center for Performance Assessment for making the publication of this work possible.

Jan would like to thank his children Zachary, Lucas, and Mahlia, and his wife, Melissa, for their continued support.

A special thank you to Allison Wedell Schumacher for editing the manuscript and for her insights and guidance in bringing this project to completion. Larry and Jan would also like to acknowledge Merle Silverman for being the first to support the publication of this work.

Preface

The Need For a "Balanced" Math Program

How can teachers build mathematically powerful students, students who can solve problems and also communicate their understanding to others? Our longtime experience as elementary and middle school math teachers has proven that when students are engaged in a "balance" of mathematics activities, they *can* succeed where it counts—in applying their math skills and reasoning ability to solve real-life problems requiring mathematical solutions. Such activities are designed to help students:

- Build computational skills

- Deepen conceptual understanding

- Develop mathematical reasoning and problem solving abilities

- Demonstrate understanding in a variety of assessment formats

We believe teachers are feeling the frustration of the times, wanting to provide their students with a strong math program, but not really feeling confident in their ability to do so. Three challenges must be addressed:

1. Many teachers have not received sufficient professional development in mathematics.

The result can be resistance to math programs that emphasize conceptual understanding over computational mastery. Without ongoing training in current methodology, these educators resort to teaching math the familiar, procedure-driven way they learned when they themselves were students.

To achieve results different from those they've been getting requires a different approach. Teachers need a new way to organize their math program—a simple framework for teaching all the essential mathematical components—and the training to confidently implement that framework.

2. Many teachers feel their district math programs are confusing, have too many components to include in an hour-long math lesson, and encompass too many units to cover in the course of one school year.

The result for these teachers can be the uncomfortable feeling that they are not doing enough, that there are too many elements to work into the lesson, and not enough time to do it all. The problem is compounded if these teachers have not received sufficient professional development to experience a paradigm shift in the way they view mathematics education, a shift that helps them:

- Encourage students to look for multiple ways to tackle a new problem

- Value students' understanding and the ability to communicate that understanding verbally and in writing

- Promote problem-solving skills over memorization of computational procedures and formulas.

In addition, many teachers perceive "holes" in their district math programs and recognize the need to supplement them with lessons and math activities from other sources. This further increases their anxiety over being able to accomplish everything students need for mathematical success.

To address this challenge, we suggest:

- An organizational structure for providing students with the necessary components of a balanced math program, regardless of the math series in use

- A template for planning instruction that aligns lessons, activities, and assessments with a math unit focus

By looking through this "balanced lens," teachers can more effectively pace their instructional activities during an hour, a week, and an entire school year. They can confidently make their own instructional decisions rather than letting the teacher's edition of the textbook drive instruction. They can more effectively utilize their district-adopted text and select supplementary materials for specific instructional purposes when appropriate. In short, they can better meet the learning needs of their students.

3. Many teachers feel pressured to make sure that their students achieve satisfactory scores on standardized achievement tests, often at the expense of teaching math in ways they know will develop their students' conceptual understanding and problem solving abilities.

Too often what results is a binary choice: either emphasize computational skills and memorization of formulas all year long in order to prepare students to do well on the standardized test *or* de-emphasize those tested skills in order to teach in-depth the lessons designed to promote conceptual understanding. Teachers who choose the latter approach often resolve their "accountability anxiety" by reluctantly putting aside their conceptual math lessons for a month prior to the test in order to "drill and kill" students on what they are likely to be tested on.

We think the solution is not the binary choice of computation *or* conceptual understanding, but rather the blend of computation *and* conceptual understanding. Such a solution may seem intellectually obvious, yet for many teachers the question remains, "*How* do I effectively combine both?" Here's how we answered that question for ourselves.

We focus on math computation practice during the first part of *every* math lesson to help students sharpen their math skills *over time*. This consistent, daily practice results in students retaining those skills long-term as opposed to the short-term recall that comes from merely cramming for the test.

We then devote the remainder of the math hour to conceptual understanding and problem solving. In this way, we prepare our students for the full range of multiple assessment measures they will encounter, from the standardized state test to all district and classroom assessments, while simultaneously providing them with the skills and understanding needed to successfully solve math-related problems throughout life.

Developing a balanced math program is the answer for teachers who want to ensure that their students are receiving the full range of mathematical understanding and skills. The purpose of this book is to share with other teachers the methods we have successfully developed for doing just this. We will take the reader step-by-step through each of the five components in our balanced math program model, describing in an easy-to-follow sequence how to implement the program successfully in the primary, intermediate, and middle school classrooms.

Contents

List of Useful Forms and Examples

Introduction

How We Came To "Balance" Our Math Program

During our years as math mentors and co-chairs of Carlsbad Unified School District's K-12 math committee in Carlsbad, California, we rode the cresting wave of change in mathematics education. In 1992, California released its new Math Framework to implement the state math standards. These rigorous standards called for significant changes in teaching practice at all grade levels. Realizing the challenges of this change, teachers and administrators began to seek answers.

Math textbook programs in use at the time emphasized computation over conceptual understanding. Math textbook publishers began scrambling to revise their forthcoming editions to emphasize conceptual understanding in order to meet the California Framework criteria and thus qualify for state adoption consideration.

During this time of transition, math teachers seemed to polarize themselves into two camps—those who chose to stay with the traditional computation-based textbook series in use and those interested in teaching mathematics conceptually.

Another factor was driving teachers to change. In addition to our annual standardized achievement test, the state had added a very different type of test to be administered later that year. The California Learning Assessment System (CLAS) test, an end-of-year math performance task given statewide in grades four, eight, and eleven, was designed to assess in-depth understanding of mathematical concepts. Almost everyone knew that our existing computation-based math series would not adequately prepare students to successfully pass the CLAS performance assessments.

In the midst of this confusion, teachers felt themselves to be in "math limbo." Many began to seek out supplemental materials emphasizing conceptual understanding and discovered "replacement units" – stand-alone units in various math strands designed to develop in-depth student understanding of critical concepts through hands-on activities.

It was clear that our colleagues needed direction, and we attempted to provide it. In our primary role as teachers, we knew we needed to redesign our own classroom math programs to address the shift in math instruction and assessment. As district math mentors, we felt a responsibility to coach teachers in effective ways to teach conceptually and prepare their students to do well on the CLAS assessments.

The Need for Professional Growth

A valuable solution presented itself in the form of the San Diego Math Project, a regional branch of the statewide California Math Project. This three-year professional development program was designed to help teachers learn how to teach math more effectively. Our participation in the SDMP helped us understand the rationale for *combining* conceptual understanding activities with computation practice and problem solving activities, and provided us with the new skills needed to translate that understanding into instructional reorganization within our own classrooms.

The SDMP familiarized us with current math research, helped us realize the importance of designing math lessons so learners could construct their own meaning, and enabled us to collaborate over time with other math teachers from districts all over the county. We became informed advocates for math reform and were able to assist our own district's teachers in learning how to implement more effective instructional and assessment practices.

Our district authorized us to purchase grade-appropriate replacement units and to provide all K-6 teachers with the training needed to use them. During these grade level workshops, we shared research-proven methods for "balancing" computational skills with conceptual understanding and problem solving that we had learned through our association with the SDMP.

The Cornerstone Question

In the summer of 1995, the K-12 math committee met to align district math standards with the new Math Framework for grades K-8. With representation from all three levels—elementary, middle school, and high school—the committee began this challenging task with a discussion about our middle school math students.

Our district's one middle school received its students from seven feeder K-6 elementary schools. Each September, incoming seventh graders displayed a wide range of mathematical understanding and ability, from very minimal to highly advanced, presenting the math teachers with a formidable challenge of meeting the instructional needs of all students.

We began our committee work that summer with a cornerstone question that started a chain reaction of insights destined to impact the way mathematics was yet to be taught.

"What foundational math skills should incoming middle school students possess?"

The responses from the committee members were immediate, the descriptions ambitious.

"These kids are coming in without a solid understanding of basic concepts such as addition, subtraction, multiplication, division, fractions, decimals, and percentages."

"And they need much more experience with geometry and measurement."

"We're having to spend too much valuable time on repetitious review of elementary concepts. We need them to be ready to take on more advanced concepts."

Heads nodded, and for a long moment, all of us were silent.

What's The Big Idea?

Someone finally asked, "So how do we do this? How do we create mathematically prepared students ready to take on middle school math concepts right out of elementary school?" The ensuing discussion led to the collective vision of a mathematically prepared middle school student, a vision that shaped our new district direction in mathematics.

We came up with the powerful idea of assigning each grade level a "Big Idea," a key mathematical number strand focus to be taught in-depth. We reasoned that if students developed a deep understanding of their current grade's Big Idea, they would not have to be re-taught the same concept over and over in subsequent years, but could build on that foundation of understanding. The Big Idea would not be the *only* math concept that a particular grade-level teacher taught, but the one for which s/he assumed instructional responsibility.

What would each grade's Big Idea be? Supported by findings from the National Council of Teachers of Mathematics (NCTM) and the California State Math Framework, we reviewed our district math standards and identified the essential number strand concept that would lay the mathematical foundation for the grade that followed. We focused our attention on K-7 only, since we knew that the eighth grade focus would be in the algebra strand. This is our list of the grade-specific Big Ideas.

Grade	Big Idea
Kindergarten	Number Sense
First Grade	Number Sense and Addition
Second Grade	Subtraction
Third Grade	Multiplication
Fourth Grade	Division
Fifth Grade	Fractions
Sixth Grade	Fractions, Decimals, and Percents
Seventh Grade	Ratio and Proportions

Aligning the Major Assessment Measures

The math committee recognized the need to show teachers:

- How to design conceptual lessons and computational skills to address the Big Idea for each grade

- How to match the grade level Big Idea with an end-of-year grade level performance task to let teachers know how successful their instruction of the Big Idea concept had been.

Designing the Balanced Math Program

We then set to work designing a K-8 math program that would combine computational skills, conceptual understanding, problem solving, mastery of basic facts, and the annual Big Idea performance task. These components came to be known as the Five Steps to a Balanced Math Program, summarized here:

Step One: **Math Review** emphasizes procedural mathematics, computational skills, and mental math, and helps prepare students for the standardized achievement test.

Step Two: **Conceptual Understanding** considers state math standards and district objectives, then identifies a unit's instructional objectives (focus statements or focus questions) and aligns instruction to assessment with an end-of-unit performance assessment evaluated with a task-specific rubric or scoring guide.

Step Three: **Problem Solving** provides both a structure for problem solving activities related to the current conceptual unit focus and a *general* problem solving rubric or scoring guide used to assess student work.

Step Four: **Mastery of Math Facts** establishes a program of accountability for mastering grade-level facts.

Step Five: **Big Idea Performance Task** identifies a number strand grade level focus K-7 that is assessed with a year-end performance task school-wide and/or district-wide.

Implementing the Program District-Wide

As the new school year began, we field-tested the program in our own classrooms. Later we conducted grade-level workshops throughout the district to introduce the five components of the balanced math program model and provide grade-specific examples. The plan won enthusiastic support with teachers and administrators because of its practicality and wide applicability across grade levels. The ideas made sense, both to the advocates of traditional math teaching methods and to those philosophically aligned with the math reform movement, and provided the missing organizational structure and format needed for teaching computation, conceptual understanding, and problem solving.

Teachers and administrators were happy to have a comprehensive plan that brought so many loose ends together and took into account the high-stakes accountability of the standardized test. We also included in our workshops practical strategies for classroom implementation.

As we continued to refine these methods with our own students in our own classrooms, we became more and more convinced that we had successfully found a way to combine the best of all worlds in mathematics instruction—the computational, the conceptual, and the practical. The balanced program worked!

What's To Follow

In Part One, we will provide both beginning and experienced teachers with a clear understanding of how to implement—*in five easy steps*—the balanced math program we have successfully developed. Each of the five chapters will end with a Reader's Assignment to help the classroom teacher prepare to implement the step just explained.

Part Two contains lesson plans and guidelines specific to the primary, intermediate, and middle school classroom. Chapters Six and Seven provide a sample three-week lesson plan for the primary (K-3) and intermediate (4-6) math classrooms, respectively. Chapter Eight addresses the unique considerations for using the balanced math program at the middle school level and includes a suggested four-week lesson plan. (Please note: we recognize that many districts house their sixth grade on elementary campuses. Sixth grade math teachers may wish to refer to both the intermediate and middle school chapters for suggestions and lesson planning.)

Chapter Nine will offer time management suggestions and practical tips for getting started that apply to all three grade spans.

An appendix containing selected blackline masters to support the program is provided at the conclusion of the book.

As We Begin

We designed *Five Easy Steps to a Balanced Math Program: A Practical Guide for Classroom Teachers* to serve as a roadmap for K-8 classroom math teachers. We encourage you to make this information your own, either by following it "to the letter" or by adapting it in whatever ways best meet your own individual needs. Our sincere hope is that our "map" will make you eager to create a balanced math program in your own classroom! If you have any questions along the way, please do not hesitate to contact either of us at the addresses provided on the How to Reach Us page at the end of the book.

PART ONE

THE

Five *Easy Steps*

CHAPTER

1

Step 1: Math Review, Computational Skills, and Mental Math

The first key component to a balanced math program is a simple system for reviewing basic computational skills that we call "Math Review." We begin the first 20 minutes of every math class with a set of five problems written on the board that students copy in their math journals and solve. These problems should:

- Reflect the computational standards for the grade level

- Match the conceptual focus of the current unit

- Provide practice in more than one math strand

- Reinforce prior learning

- Provide daily practice for the computation portion of the state and district standardized tests

Math Review is the place in the math hour to discuss with students reasonableness of answer and estimation. It is also the perfect opportunity to help students develop computational strategies and skills. Instead of teaching students an "only-one-way-to-solve-it" procedure, we emphasize and model multiple approaches to solving a problem in order to foster students' mathematical reasoning and develop their number sense.

According to Marilyn Burns, nationally recognized mathematics educator, "Number sense encompasses a wide range of abilities, including being able to make reasonable estimates, think and reason flexibly, make sound numerical judgments, and see numbers as useful. Students with number sense have good numerical intuition" (1999).

A Deliberate Progression of Concepts

An effective Math Review component to a balanced program does not come about simply by writing a different set of random arithmetic problems on the board each day. Instead, the same types of problems students see on the board on Monday reappear throughout the week. Students understand that these problems provide opportunities for practice of problems they have already been introduced to, and that they may receive additional guidance and instruction as needed from either their teacher or their peers.

Students also understand that their progress will be assessed weekly by encountering the same kinds of problems on the Friday Math Review quiz. If we want students to maximize their learning of particular math computational skills, it is necessary to avoid introducing them to new kinds of problems within the same week and to instead provide them with consistent practice of the same types of problems until they are learned.

Math Review presents a deliberate progression of mathematical concepts and computational skills that increase in difficulty throughout the school year. Problems of the same type recur week after week until the majority of the class masters them. Only then does the teacher introduce a new concept or skill, which replaces the one the students have sufficiently learned. In this way, new types of problems are cycled through Math Review as the year proceeds.

If students need to review any concepts at some point later in the year, those types of problems can again be included in Math Review. However, if students practice a particular computational skill until they thoroughly understand it, it becomes less likely that they will need to be re-taught that skill in the future. They can later revisit skills and concepts and build on prior understanding.

The Math Review Template

The Math Review Template shown on the next page is an organizational structure we developed to facilitate this daily computational practice. It consists of five labeled rectangles targeting the current five math skills the teacher wants his or her students to focus on learning that week.

For example, at the beginning of fifth grade, the Template targets the five categories listed below. An explanation of how we instruct students to solve these problems as well as how we process the problems together at the end of Math Review will be discussed in the sections that follow.

Fifth Grade Math Review Template

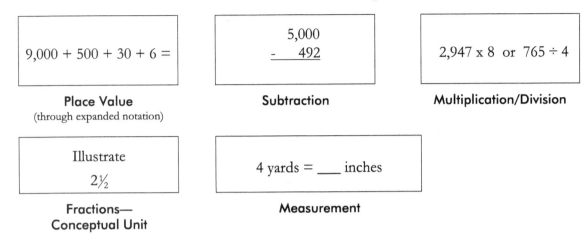

9,000 + 500 + 30 + 6 =

Place Value
(through expanded notation)

5,000
-     492

Subtraction

2,947 x 8 or 765 ÷ 4

Multiplication/Division

Illustrate

2½

**Fractions—
Conceptual Unit**

4 yards = ___ inches

Measurement

The scope of this book does not allow for a full year's inclusion of Math Review problems for every grade level, but the primary, intermediate, and middle school classroom chapters in Part Two each contain a three- or four-week Math Review lesson plan for beginning the year. These lesson plans will provide the reader with a model from which to proceed in subsequent weeks.

The Teacher's Role During Math Review

The teacher's role is critical to the success of Math Review. Students need to hear the teacher giving such encouragement as, "Math Review is a time for *practice*. We are all trying to get better at this, so let's help each other as much as possible."

While the students are working, the teacher circulates throughout the classroom and invites those having difficulty with a particular problem to come forward to the board for individual or small group assistance. Students can come and go after each problem, depending on their needs. These changing, informal groups, called "flex groups," provide a safe place for students to seek the help they might otherwise not ask for. The teacher strives to create a collaborative atmosphere in which kids are willing to risk and admit their need for help. The message is, "Learning is a process that begins with *not* knowing. As we practice and help each other, we come to understand."

Tutors and Tutees

Another successful method we use to build a supportive classroom atmosphere and meet the varying needs of all students is "Tutors and Tutees," a student-student partnership so named by a colleague of ours, Scott Koopsen, who teaches fifth grade in Carlsbad, CA. The tutors are peer helpers who volunteer to provide free advice sessions during Math Review, at recess, or even during lunch, for "tutees," those students who are struggling with one or more computational skills.

Very often students can learn computational strategies more effectively from their peers than from their teachers. Having tutors helping tutees also provides teachers with needed assistance when many students are asking for help at the same time. Because the teacher has organized Math Review to take advantage of students' ability to assist one another, students who need help get help when they need it and are less likely to mathematically "fall through the cracks" as the year progresses.

It is important to note that tutors who can successfully solve the Math Review problems are also challenged to do more advanced work, and not just become teacher aides. Students proficient at Math Review can certainly deepen their own understanding of mathematical concepts and skills by coaching their peers, but they must also be encouraged to tackle new problems that challenge them.

One way the teacher can challenge these students is to put one or more "bonus" problems on the board for them to attempt. These bonus problems closely relate to the computational focus of the five problems the class is practicing during any given week, but they are more rigorous and extend student understanding of those kinds of problems.

Processing Math Review

When the majority of students have finished solving the five Math Review problems, it is time to correct the problems together. The key to processing Math Review effectively is to emphasize *number sense* and *reasonableness of answer*. In other words, the goal is to help students determine whether their answer is reasonable in the context of the particular problem and if it demonstrates an understanding of our number system.

When teachers have successfully created a classroom climate where mistakes are regarded as a normal part of the learning process, it is much easier to teach their students how to do an "error analysis" when Math Review answers are incorrect. We define "error analysis" as helping students (1) identify the part of the problem done correctly and (2) pinpoint the part of the problem where they made an error.

There are several ways to process Math Review and conduct such an error analysis. The teacher can select the method that best meets the changing needs of the class. Here are a few of the ways we process Math Review and teach error analysis:

1. **Teacher-directed.** When introducing a new concept or when a majority of the class seems stuck on a particular problem, the teacher may lead the class through the step-by-step computational procedure, pointing out the critical elements, and asking students for a reasonable answer (one that makes sense). Students are encouraged to take notes on key points to help them remember how to solve the problem on their own the next time they encounter a similar problem.

2. **Student-directed.** In this method, student volunteers talk the class through the procedure they themselves followed to arrive at a solution to each of the five Math Review problems. If other students have a different approach to reach the same solution on a particular problem, and the teacher decides it would benefit the rest of the class to see it, s/he may invite those students to share their approach as well.

3. **"Pass the Chalk."** This is a diagnostic tool we use when most of the students know how to do a particular kind of problem. It is an effective method to assist the teacher in seeing where students might have trouble with a particular part of a problem and to provide needed instruction. As one student demonstrates one step of the solution on the board, others watch to see if they agree or disagree. The student then "passes the chalk" to another student who must provide the next step. This continues until the problem is solved and all agree that it is correct.

4. **Speedy System.** When students have become successful with the Math Review problems, volunteers go to the board and just write the answer to the problem. They then ask the class, "How many agree? How many disagree?" This enables the class to determine quickly whether their answers are correct or not.

One cautionary note: Math Review provides such stimulating opportunities for teacher instruction and student learning that it can easily expand to encompass the entire time allocated for math! In the beginning of the year, or when introducing a new concept for students to practice, the time required is naturally longer. But strive to keep Math Review and Mental Math (described in the next section) to about one-third of the entire math session. Otherwise, the first step in our balanced math program will "unbalance" the other four!

Mental Math

The second part of Step One is Mental Math, a three-problem, computational workout for the brain that students love doing. Mental Math takes about five minutes of class time and immediately follows the processing of the Math Review problems.

The purpose of Mental Math is to provide students with *mental* practice in computing basic number facts and combining mathematical operations. The teacher dictates a string of numbers and operations that students compute mentally to determine the final answer.

For example, the teacher calls out the number string, "2 x 4 + 8 − 6 ÷ 2," pausing briefly after each operational step, so that it sounds something like this: "Two times four...plus eight...minus six...divided by two." At each pause, students have a chance to calculate mentally before the teacher moves on to the next step, but they don't write anything down until the final answer. In the example above, students calculate the answer in their heads and write "5" (hopefully) in their math journals right beneath the Math Review problems of the day.

The answer is not given yet, however. The teacher repeats the same problem to allow students who might need a second chance to succeed. Those who think they know the correct answer are asked to calculate again to make sure. The teacher then asks the students to announce the solution, and the answer is verified by computing the problem aloud in increments to help those remaining students who were still unable to do it. In this way, everyone stays involved.

We usually can accomplish three Mental Math problems in five to seven minutes once the students are familiar with the procedure. As students become more adept at Mental Math, problems can be lengthened and made more challenging.

Students often want to create their own Mental Math problems to dictate to the rest of the class. We always encourage this kind of involvement. However, before allowing these volunteers to say their problem aloud, we require them to write out their number string and have it checked by us for appropriateness of difficulty (sometimes it's too long and convoluted). We've also found it a good practice to write down the problem before dictating it aloud to the students. More than once, we've been unable to repeat the number string exactly, causing a minor uproar in the classroom!

Mental Math Benefits

Practice doesn't always make perfect, but doing Mental Math daily throughout the school year helps all students demonstrate dramatic improvement. It provides students with regular opportunities to apply properties and patterns of our number system. Consider this number string: "Start with 3 + 1; take the square root of the number and multiply it by 100; take three quarters of that answer; multiply that by zero; subtract the number of hours in two days; find the absolute value of that. Answer?" In this Mental Math number string, students are reinforcing their understanding of:

- Multiplying a number by 10, 100, or 1000

- Multiplying or dividing a number by zero

- Number facts (addition, subtraction, multiplication, division)

- Fractional parts

- Math vocabulary

- Square root and absolute value

- Measurement concepts (number of days in a week, month, year; number of hours in two, three, or more days; number of inches in a foot, in three feet, etc.).

Many excellent commercial sources for Mental Math are available, but we find that teachers enjoy making them up themselves once they become familiar with the process. Examples of Mental Math problems have been included in each of the primary, intermediate, and middle school classroom implementation chapters to provide a model for doing so.

Accountability: The Math Review Quiz

The Math Review Quiz provides the means for determining which students do and do not understand the computational problems they've been practicing throughout the week. Each Friday, a ten-problem quiz consisting of two problems for each of the five kinds of problems practiced is given to all students. Students need to correctly solve eight out of the ten problems on the Math Review Quiz to pass it. Students who demonstrate this level of proficiency on the quiz may, in the next week, choose to do only the bonus problems provided daily or assist other students as tutors. But these students must take the following Friday's quiz to show that they can still correctly solve these same kinds of problems. Once new types of problems are "cycled in," all students will complete the daily Math Review practice problems.

The Home Connection and Extra Practice

Students take home their graded Math Review Quiz for parents to review and sign. This weekly accountability informs parents of the actual progress their child is making in math computation. If students score less than 80%, their parents help them with assigned homework problems like those missed on the quiz.

Each morning, the teacher quickly checks to see if students have completed and returned the homework problems. By consistently monitoring the completion of this extra practice, the teacher communicates high expectations and establishes a standard of accountability to students.

During Math Review, the teacher works with these same students one-on-one or in a small flex group to make sure they receive additional instruction and assistance. This combined effort—the teacher providing extra help during Math Review and the parents helping their children at home—has proven quite successful for students who struggle with computation.

When help at home is not possible for certain students, we have matched those students with peers, parent volunteers, or teacher aides who help them practice at school. Depending on the unique circumstances at each school, the teachers and administrators must determine their own kind of internal support system for helping these students before, during, and/or after the regular school day.

Benefits of the Math Review Quiz

The Math Review Quiz provides the teacher with a weekly assessment that:

- Identifies those students needing more individualized attention

- Gauges the effectiveness of computational instruction

If only a few students score below 80%, those children can be taught individually or in small groups until they improve. If a majority of the class falls below the 80% score, the teacher needs to reevaluate the ways s/he is presenting instruction during Math Review and to make adjustments accordingly. In this way, assessment serves its most important function, that of informing instruction.

Examples of Friday quizzes aligned to weekly Math Review problems are included in the classroom implementation chapters of Part II.

Reader's Assignments

Rather than waiting until the end of this book to begin planning how to implement these suggestions for creating a balanced math program in your own classroom, you may wish to put this information immediately to use and "plan as you go." We have therefore included a reader's assignment at the end of each of the five steps to guide you (and your grade level or math department colleagues) through the step-by-step process of planning your own balanced program.

Step One
Reader's Assignment

Plan your own grade-level Math Review Template and Mental Math problems. Refer to the specific classroom chapter (Six, Seven, or Eight) that is closest to the grade you teach. There you will find a sample lesson plan of suggested Math Review and Mental Math problems for the first few weeks of the school year.

CHAPTER

2

Step 2: Conceptual Understanding

Developing students' conceptual understanding is at the heart of effective mathematics instruction. The second step of a balanced math program is designed to help teachers, working alone or collaboratively, to prepare a conceptual unit aimed at deepening student understanding of that unit's central mathematical focus.

Writing curriculum and designing units of study is time-intensive work, best done in collaboration with one or more grade-level or department colleagues. Whether done before the start of a new school year, or completed throughout the year as needed, it takes time to think deeply about the essential understandings we want students to develop. Yet this investment of time yields one of the classroom teachers' best returns—planned instruction and assessment that leads to greater student understanding.

Teaching is in many respects still an isolated profession. Teachers rarely receive the valuable opportunity to collaborate with colleagues. Whatever instructional planning they do is usually done alone and on their own time. Yet we know the power of two or more teachers gathered together to plan cooperatively. We see this collaboration as a critical need for schools and districts serious about implementing instructional change.

Teachers belong at the center of all instructional decisions. When encouraged to use their experience and knowledge of subject matter to develop curricular focus, they create powerful learning experiences for students.

Designing A Conceptual Unit

The Conceptual Understanding step is the portion of the math hour where students engage in a lesson or activity as part of a math unit that is several weeks long. It follows Math Review and Mental Math and requires approximately 35-45 minutes to complete. Here is an overview of the sequence we follow when designing a conceptual unit. This sequence will be discussed in detail in the sections below:

1. Establish the focus for the unit: Exactly what do you want students to learn?

2. Determine an end-of-unit performance task (an *applied demonstration* of what students have learned in relation to the unit focus).

3. Plan all of the unit's instructional activities guided by the unit focus.

4. Teach the unit according to this plan.

5. Create the rubric or scoring guide to assess the performance task, then assign the performance task.

6. Peer-, self-, and teacher-assess the completed performance task with the scoring guide.

7. Ask students to write a self-reflection about their learning in relation to the unit focus.

8. Compile and grade a unit folder of all assignments, homework, quizzes, and the performance task.

9. Spend a few moments engaged in your own self-reflection.

1. Establish the focus for the unit.

Working with your grade level colleagues, determine the focus of the unit you're preparing to teach by considering district and state math standards and by examining the more detailed descriptions of what students are to learn at your particular grade level (named benchmarks, proficiencies, learning expectations, etc.). Then write those key unit concepts in the form of *focus statements* or *focus questions* following the process described below.

In planning a unit together, grade level colleagues ask, "What three or four critical concepts and skills do we want the students to understand and be able to apply when this unit of study is completed?" This question and the ensuing discussion to determine the essential focus of the unit are extremely important. They help the participating teachers clarify what's important in the content they are preparing to teach.

Grant Wiggins and Jay McTighe refer to this process as "backwards design:" "One starts with the end—the desired results (goals or standards)—and then derives the curriculum from the evidence of learning (performances) called for by the standard and the teaching needed to equip students to perform" (1998).

Because students are the ones most involved in the learning process, some teachers like to ask students what questions *they* have about a particular topic before beginning the unit. The teachers can then consider these questions along with their state and district standards when formally deciding the unit's focus. Teachers often prefer writing these key concepts for the unit as questions rather than statements because they have found that an inquiry-based format better engages the interest of their students.

For example, before finalizing the unit focus statements or questions for a division unit, fourth grade teachers asked their students what they wanted to know about division. This is a sampling of what the students answered:

• Do multiplication and division work together like addition and subtraction?

• How do you know when to divide in real life?

• Is there more than one way to do division?

The final focus statements or questions for the unit do much more than just let students know what they will be learning or what their teacher will be teaching. They serve as an instructional tool for teachers to use in deciding which lessons and activities are necessary to develop student understanding around the key unit concepts. They enable the teachers to determine if the text materials meet the targeted unit focus or whether supplemental materials are needed. If other resources need to be explored, the teachers again apply the filter of the unit focus when selecting those materials.

Below are the focus questions for a subtraction unit in a second grade classroom, a division unit in a fourth grade classroom, and a ratio/proportion/percent unit in a seventh grade math program.

It's interesting to note that the fourth grade teachers chose to write focus *statements*, but in reflecting on the unit after its completion, they wished they had formulated them as questions. The *essence* of what students wanted to learn (refer again to the three questions listed above) closely matched the teachers' ideas about what key concepts to target. The question format, they concluded, seemed more instructionally motivational.

Second Grade Subtraction Unit

Focus Question:

1. How do ones, tens, and hundreds work together?

Fourth Grade Division Unit

Focus Statements:

1. Show different ways to solve a division problem.

2. Write a math story to illustrate a division problem.

3. Show the relationship between multiplication and division.

Seventh Grade Ratio/Proportion/Percent Unit

Focus Statements:

1. Write ratios in simplest form and as unit rates.

2. Find probability of simple events.

3. Use proportion to solve problems.

4. Use percent to solve problems.

2. Determine the performance task (end-of-unit assessment).

A suitable performance task to assess conceptual understanding should be one that affords students the opportunity to demonstrate their full range of understanding of the concept. We make certain that the assessment task matches the unit focus statements or questions and is aligned with all lessons and activities presented during the course of the unit. A review of available resources (the math series in use, supplemental materials, etc.) will enable the teachers to select or modify a suitable assessment. If one can't be found in published materials, teachers simply create their own.

The end-of-unit performance task *does not replace* the more traditional quizzes or tests that the teacher administers during the course of the unit to assess students' formative understanding of the focus questions. Ideally, the performance task provides students with a more open-ended opportunity to demonstrate the *application* of the content and skills they have learned. The essential requirement in designing a performance task is to align it to the unit focus statements or questions so that the student's summative understanding of the unit focus can be determined.

In the following pages are three examples of teacher-created performance task assessments matched to the focus statements or questions for the second, fourth, and seventh grade math units listed previously. The accompanying student work can be found immediately following the scoring guides used to assess those performance tasks, all of which appear later in the chapter. By including the student work there, the reader can see how the rubric matched the performance task requirements.

Second Grade Subtraction Unit

Performance Task

1. Play the "Ones, Tens, and Hundreds" game using the game board, dice, and base ten blocks.

2. Use words, pictures, and numbers to show how ones and tens are regrouped.

3. Use words, pictures, and numbers to show how tens and hundreds are regrouped.

Fourth Grade Division Unit

Performance Task

1. Solve $104 \div 8$ using repeated subtraction. Show your work.

2. Solve $104 \div 8$ using repeated addition. Show your work.

3. Solve $104 \div 8$ using guess and check. Show your work.

4. Solve $104 \div 8$ using either the multiples method or the standard algorithm for long division. Show your work.

5. Prove your answer for $104 \div 8$ using multiplication. How do you know your quotient is correct?

6. Make up a math story that matches this division problem, $104 \div 8$. Label your numbers with words. Show the answer, too.

Seventh Grade Ratio/Proportion/Percent Unit

Performance Task

The Runners' Dilemma

Caroline is chasing after Sam. They are 80 feet apart. Sam runs at a speed of 22 feet per second and Caroline runs at a speed of 31 feet per second. How many seconds will it take for Caroline to catch Sam? Think of a way to represent your findings. Explain your thinking fully.

3. Plan the unit activities and instruction guided by the unit focus.

With your grade level colleagues, review the math series and any supplemental materials and decide the unit activities to advance students' mathematical understanding of the unit focus statements or questions.

When reviewing materials and resources for the unit's design, the most helpful question to frame your review is, "Will this activity or lesson advance understanding of the focus of the unit?" If it does, great! If it doesn't, determine if it could be modified so that it does. If the answer is no, continue searching for those resources that will.

This single guiding question serves two important functions. First, it acts as an instructional filter, allowing the teacher to successfully streamline the unit by selecting only those activities that advance student understanding of the unit focus, and second, it promotes the alignment of curriculum, instruction, and assessment.

4. Teach the unit.

Begin each math unit by presenting to the students the focus statements or questions for that unit. This lets the students know plainly what they are to learn. Direct students to copy these focus statements or questions onto paper. Then, tell them what you have planned for the performance task at the conclusion of the unit so they will know *in advance* how they will be assessed. Strive to present your instruction and the assignments students complete in a format similar to the one you've selected for the end-of-unit performance task.

At the conclusion of the first lesson or activity, start an ongoing table of contents with the students on a piece of easel-size chart paper. Each time a paper activity is concluded (including homework, class assignments, formative quizzes, and tests), add the title of that activity to the table of contents and direct the students to copy it onto their own individual table of contents page.

Upper elementary and middle school teachers instruct their students to keep all the completed work for the unit in the math section of their binders, letting students know that all completed work will eventually comprise the end-of-unit math folder. Primary teachers help their students organize and keep their work in the classroom throughout the course of the unit.

Whenever possible, present the selected activities and lessons in a hands-on approach that helps students build their own understanding of the unit focus statements or questions. Remember to incorporate into Math Review and Mental Math the computational skills that relate to the conceptual understanding the students are developing.

Students complete the conceptual lessons and activities individually, in pairs, cooperatively in teams, and/or together as a class. Often we only evaluate these formative activities for completion and demonstration of students' current level of understanding, using this feedback to modify and improve our own instruction.

We believe that students need the opportunity to wrestle with mathematical ideas to construct personal meaning. Here, *depth of understanding* is the goal, as opposed to assessment of each little practice step along the way. We recognize the need to review with students the answers to problems they have done in class and to process together their homework. We know we must periodically check for student understanding through formative assessments of critical content and skills. However, we made a conscious decision to personally stop grading every single paper that each student completes when the class is in the practice phase of learning the concepts in focus. We now reserve our grading time for Math Review quizzes, formative assessments of the unit concept, the end-of-unit performance task, and the grading of the unit folder.

5. Create a scoring guide or rubric to assess unit performance task.

A scoring guide, or rubric, is used to assess the end-of-unit performance task. It can be teacher-designed or student-created under the guidance of the classroom teacher. This scoring guide contains *specific* descriptors that let students know exactly what they need to do to demonstrate proficiency on the performance task.

Create the rubric *before* students begin working on the performance task so that they know how their performance will be evaluated before they ever begin working on it. Establishing clear-cut criteria in advance of doing the work helps students better understand the performance task directions and enables them to set personal goals for achieving the grade they wish to earn. The rubric levels can be labeled with letters, numbers, words, or symbols. Lower primary grades often use a star, happy face, straight face or different colors. Use whatever labels work best for student understanding.

How many performance levels should a rubric contain? Six? Four? Three? Two? This is a decision to be made locally—by the district, school, department, grade, or individual classroom. As a general rule-of-thumb, we recommend a four-level scoring guide for upper elementary and middle school math performance tasks, and a three-level scoring guide for primary grades. Rubrics with five and six levels often become too subtle in the distinctions between the levels, making it difficult for students (and even teachers!) to understand the differences between them.

The greatest success we have had in beginning the design of a scoring guide with students is to completely explain the task directions to the class and then ask, "What would 'proficient' look like?" Students discuss and agree upon the objective criteria that must be present in a student's paper or project to be considered "proficient" by anyone looking at that paper or project. Invariably the students suggest specifically worded criteria that directly match the requirements of the performance task. To receive a grade of "proficient" (or whatever label term corresponds to "proficient" in colors, numbers, words, or letters), students need to show evidence that they have fulfilled the scoring guide's specific description of what "proficient" means.

To receive a grade of "exemplary," (or whatever label term corresponds to "exemplary" in colors, numbers, words, or letters), students need to show evidence that they have demonstrated greater quantity and/or quality, that they have gone "above and beyond" the requirements for proficient performance. The rubric must specify these qualitative and quantitative descriptors in language all students understand.

The best way to explain quality is by showing examples of it. It is imperative to provide students with exemplars or models of both proficient and exemplary work, such as benchmark papers. This is an essential part of helping students make the connection between *written descriptions* of quality and proficiency and *visible demonstrations* of quality and proficiency specific to the performance task requirements.

Many teachers begin writing a scoring guide by starting from the top score and working their way down, starting with the "3" paper, for example, and subtracting quality and quantity descriptors to agree upon the "2" paper and then the "1" paper. Others like to begin with the bottom score and work their way up. Most teachers report that they prefer starting with the "proficient" category because that's the level of performance they expect from their students. They then follow with the "exemplary," the "progressing," and the "not yet meeting standards" categories. We encourage teachers to use whichever method and approach makes the most sense to them and their students.

Once the criteria for each of the performance levels have been written, revised, shared with, and agreed upon by all members of the classroom, the rubric is typed and distributed. Students use the scoring guide as travelers use a roadmap, referring to it throughout the completion of their performance task to arrive at the "destination" of proficient work.

The procedure for involving all students in designing scoring guides is described fully in our book, *Student Generated Rubrics: An Assessment Model to Help All Students Succeed* (1998). Additional information is provided in the next chapter, Problem Solving and Math Application, that describes how students and teacher create a general rubric that can be used all year long to assess the weekly Problem-of-the-Week.

Included in the following pages are the student-generated rubrics that were designed to evaluate the second, fourth, and seventh grade performance tasks cited earlier in this chapter. They are followed by examples of student work on the corresponding performance tasks.

Note the use of the term "kinda" in the second grade rubric. This word, although subjective in terms of what it might mean to most, was completely understandable to the second graders in this particular class. In general, we advocate only the use of objective and measurable descriptors in each of the performance levels of a rubric. However, as long as there is clear consensus among the students—derived from examples to demonstrate a term's meaning—a subjective word or phrase can be used.

In the fourth grade student-generated rubric, you'll find that certain criteria between the four grading categories overlap or contradict one another. (Can you identify any criteria that might be confusing for students to use?) The teacher in whose classroom this rubric was designed didn't notice this until peer-assessment had begun. He decided, however, to stay with the rubric as written rather than cause confusion by unilaterally changing it midstream. He helped students resolve individual questions or uncertainties as they occurred during the grading process.

The teacher told us that this "mistake" had proven a valuable learning experience for him in terms of leading future rubric-writing sessions with his students. He realized that the more grading levels the rubric contained, the more difficulty students had in authoring the rubric and distinguishing between the different criteria descriptors during the grading process. A three-point rubric would have been more "user-friendly." He again reiterated the necessity of reviewing the finished rubric to make certain that criteria do not overlap or conflict with each other *before* publishing it and using it with students.

Student Generated Rubric for
Second Grade Subtraction Unit Performance Task

"3"

- Picture has words, pictures, and numbers
- Reader can understand how ones, tens, and hundreds work together
- Pictures are about the math in the problem

"2"

- Picture has words, pictures, and numbers
- Reader can "kinda" understand how ones, tens, and hundreds work together (definition of "kinda" understood by entire class)
- Pictures are about the math in the problem

"1"

- Picture has words, pictures, or numbers
- Reader cannot understand how ones, tens, and hundreds work together
- Pictures are *not* about the math in the problem

Second Grade Performance Task

Assignment Directions: Draw a picture to show how ones and tens are regrouped. Then draw a picture to show how tens and hundreds are regrouped.

The ones, tens, hundreds game   by Staci

Hundreds	Tens	Ones
		• • • • • •

This is about a ones, tens, and hundreds game. If you roll a seven you need to put seven spots in the ones bos.

Hundreds	Tens	Ones
		• • • • • • • • • • •

Then if you roll the dice and get a four you need to put four more in the ones box. Now you have eleven in the ones box.

Hundreds	Tens	Ones
	• • • • • • • • • •	•

You have to move ten of them to the tens box, and leave the one there. Ten ones in the tens box is called a rod.

Hundreds	Tens	Ones
• •		•

Later on, if you get ten rods in the tens box then you have a hundred and you have to move it to the hundreds box like this.

Student Generated Rubric for
Fourth Grade Division Unit Performance Task

E

- Correct answers on all 6 problems
- Math is correct on every problem
- Every solution is complete and makes sense

S+

- Correct answers on only 3 "different ways to solve" problems
- Multiplication and division relationship problem is correct
- 1-2 calculation mistakes

S

- Correct answer on only 2 "different ways to solve" problems
- Correct answer on multiplication and division relationship problem OR math story problem
- 3-4 calculation mistakes
- Solutions hard to understand or incomplete

S-

- Correct answer on only 1 "different ways to solve" problems
- Correct answer on multiplication and division relationship problem OR math story problem
- 5 or more calculation mistakes
- One or two problems the person didn't do

Peer Graders _____ and _____

Peer Grade _____ because_____

Self-Grade _____ because _____

Teacher"s Grade _____ because _____

Fourth Grade Division Unit Performance Task

Name _Kelly_____ Date _4-26-2000_____

Focus Statement: Show different ways to solve a division problem.

1. Solve 104 ÷ 8 using repeated subtraction. Show your work.

   104(-8)=96 96(-8)=88 88(-8)=80 80(-8)=72 72(-8)=64 64(-8)=5
   6 56(-8)=48 48(-8)=40 40(-8)=32 32(-8)=24 24(-8)=16 16(-8)=8
   8(-8)=0
   Quotient is 13 (because I subtracted 8 thirteen times).

2. Solve 104 ÷ 8 using repeated addition. Show your work.

   0(+8)=8 8(+8)=16 16(+8)=24 24(+8)=32 32(+8)=40 40(+8)=48
   48(+8)=56 56(+8)=64 64(+8)=72 72+8=80 80(+8)=88 88(+8)=96
   96(+8)=104
   Quotient is 13 (because I circled +8 thirteen times so I know that
   104 ÷ 8 is 13).

3. Solve 104 ÷ 8 using guess and check. Show your work.

   Guess 100 ÷ 10=10   8x10=80 too low
                              8x12=96 a little better
                              8x14=112 too high
                              8x13=104 just right   Quotient is 13.

4. Solve 104 ÷ 8 using either standard algorithm method or multiples method.

   ```
     013
   8)104        Quotient is 13, but I can solve it with multiples, too.
     -8         8, 16, 24, 32, 40, 48, 56, 64, 72, 80, 88, 96, 104.
     024
     -24
       0
   ```

Name __Kelly__   Date __4-26-2000__

Focus Statement: Show different ways to solve a division problem.

5. Prove your answer for 104 ÷ 8 using multiplication.
   How do you know your quotient is correct?

   $8 \times 13 = 104$ because

   | 13 |
   | 13 |
   | 13 |
   | 13 |
   | 13 |
   | 13 |
   | 13   There are eight 13's. |
   | + 13 |
   | 104 |

6. Make up a math story that matches this division problem: 104 ÷ 8
   Label your numbers with words. Show the answer, too.

   I went to a birthday party with hungry kids. I brought along 104 cupcakes
   for the 8 kids at the party. How many cupcakes will each kid get?

   Estimate _____

   Quotient: 104 ÷ 8 = 13

Student Generated Rubric for Seventh Grade Ratio, Proportion, and Percent Performance Task

A

- Correct Answer
- Explanation matches data sheet
- Clear mathematical reasoning
- Explanation shows use of ratio, unit rates, or proportion to solve problem
- All write-up guide requirements complete

B

- Correct Answer
- Explanation matches data sheet
- Clear mathematical reasoning
- Explanation shows use of ratio, unit rates, or proportion to solve problem
- 1-2 items missing from the write-up guide

C

- Correct or incorrect answer
- Explanation does not match data sheet
- Mathematical reasoning unclear
- Explanation does not show use of ratio, unit rates, or proportion to solve problem
- 3-4 items missing from the write-up guide

D

- Incorrect answer
- Data sheet missing
- More than 4 items missing from the write-up guide

Seventh Grade Ratio/Proportion/Percent Unit

Performance Task: The Runners' Dilemma

Caroline is chasing after Sam. They are 80 feet apart. Sam runs at a speed of 22 feet per second and Caroline runs at a speed of 31 feet per second. How many seconds will it take for Caroline to catch Sam? Think of a way to represent your findings. Explain your thinking fully.

Brad   May 3, 2000
Period 4

Caroline · · · · · · · · · · · · · · 80 feet · · · · · · · · · · · · · · · Sam
0   (80-0=80)   +80
+31   After 1 second   +22
Caroline · · · · · · · · · · · · · 71 feet · · · · · · · · · · · Sam
31   (102-31=71)   102
+31   After 2 seconds   +22
Caroline · · · · · · · · · · · · 62 feet · · · · · · · · · · · Sam
62   (124-62=62)   124
+31   After 3 seconds   +22
Caroline · · · · · · · · · · · 53 feet · · · · · · · · · · Sam
93   (146-93=53)   146
+31   After 4 seconds   +22
Caroline · · · · · · · · · · 44 feet · · · · · · · · · Sam
124   (168-124=44)   168
+31   After 5 seconds   +22
Caroline · · · · · · · · · 35 feet · · · · · · · · Sam
155   (190-155=35)   190
+31   After 6 seconds   +22
Caroline · · · · · · · · 26 feet · · · · · · · Sam
186   (212-186=26)   212
+31   After 7 seconds   +22
Caroline · · · · 17 feet · · · · · · · · · · Sam
217   (234-217=17)   234
+31   After 8 seconds   +22
Caroline · · · · · 8 feet · · · · · · Sam
248   (256-248=8)   256

8 ÷9=.88   Answer: 8.88 seconds
Another way: 31 (caroline)-22 (Sam) = 9
               80 feet ÷ 9 feet per second = 8.88 seconds

Brad   May 3, 2000
Period 4

Performance Task: The Runner's Dilemma

1. Problem Statement: Two runners start at the same time, with Sam
    starting 80 feet ahead of Caroline. Sam runs at 22 feet per second
    and Caroline runs at 31 feet per second. How many seconds will it
    take for Caroline to catch up to Sam?

2. Plan: I will use pictures and graphs to help me solve the problem.
    I estimate that it will take Caroline 10 seconds to catch Sam.

3. Work Section: First I drew some diagrams showing the distance in
    feet between Caroline and Sam. I added 31 feet to Caroline's side,
    and 22 feet to Sam's side after each second. When it reached 8
    seconds, I knew that in 9 seconds Caroline would have passed Sam,
    so I divided 8 by 9 to get .88 seconds, and added that to the 8
    seconds to get 8.88 seconds.

    I also tried another way to make sure my answer was correct. I
    subtracted 31 (Caroline's feet per second) and 22 (Sam's feet per
    second) to get 9, which I divided into 80 (the distance between Sam
    and Caroline), and I got 8.88 seconds, which was my first answer.

4. Answer section: My answer is 8.88 seconds. That is 1.22 seconds
    less than my estimate, which was 10 seconds. I know my answer is
    correct because 31 (Caroline's fps) times 8.88 is 275.55, and so is
    22 (Sam's fps) times 8.8, plus the 80 feet ahead that he started out
    in front of Caroline.

6. Peer-, self-, and teacher-assess the completed performance task with the scoring guide.

At the completion of the performance task, intermediate and middle school students use their scoring guide or rubric to assess first the work of their peers and then their own work. Primary students typically evaluate only their own work. (This is not a hard and fast rule, but is a decision left to primary teachers based on the maturity of their individual classes). The teacher reviews the peer-graders' evaluations and the individual students' evaluations. Then, using the same rubric, s/he makes the final grade determination. This is an important distinction to make to parents to assure them that their child's work will be evaluated by the teacher, and not by other students only.

Teaching students to peer-assess and self-assess is a critical piece of creating a student-centered assessment program. If students help write the rubric, and are then left out of the actual evaluation of the performance tasks, they don't make the same kind of connection between the rubric and its direct correlation with the final grade they receive. Because our goal is to de-mystify the grading process for students, we involve them in the actual assessment of their completed performance tasks so they can make that vital connection.

Before the actual grading begins, the teacher leads the class in an "anchoring" session, whereby s/he reviews the scoring guide criteria with the students. The teacher reads aloud sample student performance tasks or invites volunteer students to do the same. The teacher leads the class in identifying the required elements listed on the scoring guide that are included in the student's work. Any omissions are also identified. The grade for the performance task is thus determined based on the rubric criteria met.

When the teacher is satisfied that students can correctly use the rubric to evaluate student work, s/he assigns grading partners and gives each pair another student's performance task to assess. The teacher directs the student partnerships to check off the scoring guide criteria that are present and to use a colored highlighter to accent the criteria not met. These student partnerships complete their evaluation in the space provided on the attached scoring guide and return to the teacher to have their evaluation reviewed. If the students have completed the evaluation correctly, they then receive another student's work to evaluate. If not, the teacher points out whatever needs to be evaluated again, and the students return to their desks to do that. Suggestions for partnering students and guidelines for paper flow procedures, as well as for teaching students how to write appropriate feedback comments based on the rubric, can be found in Chapter Three.

When all papers or projects have been peer-graded, the students receive their own work, review the peer-grade, and then evaluate their own work in the space provided on the scoring guide. When finished, students submit their performance tasks to the teacher for the final grade determination.

We advocate giving students more than one opportunity to demonstrate proficiency on a performance task. The scoring guide is a tool for helping students understand and reach proficiency. For many students, this proficiency does not occur the first time around. Yet at some point, the final grade must be determined and recorded. Teachers need to decide for themselves to what extent students can use the scoring guide feedback to revise their work before they make the final grade determination.

7. Engage students in self-reflection.

After returning the graded performance tasks to the students, the teacher asks the class to respond to one, two, or three self-reflection questions. These questions are designed to help students determine to what degree they learned the unit focus statements or focus questions and to identify specific areas in which they see the need to improve. The teacher also asks students to determine a specific plan for improvement during the next math unit.

On the following pages are the self-reflections of the second, fourth, and seventh graders concerning the division unit focus statements and their completed performance task and evaluation.

Second Grade Subtraction Unit

Name _Staci_____ Date ___4-26-2000_____

Ones, Tens, Hundreds Reflection

1. What did you learn about subtraction and regrouping?

> I learned that you can trade ten cubes for one rod.
>
> I learned that you can trade ten rods for one flat.
>
> But if there are any left over in each group you have to leave them where they are.
>
> Subtraction is fun!

Fourth Grade Division Unit

Name ___Kelly_____ Date ___4-26-2000___

Self-Reflection

1. Which way(s) to solve a division problem made the most sense to you? Why?

    To find out the answer of division I like to use multiples. I take a problem and go like this: 8, 16, 24, 32, 40, 48, 56, 64, and so on. Then I count the multiples and that gives me the answer. I like multiples because they are fun and easy. Example: $104 \div 8 = 13$. I know this because I can count how many multiples there are in the eights to get to 104. I go like this: 8, 16, 24, 32, 40, 48, 56, 64, 72, 80, 88, 96, and 104. That's 13 multiples or 13 groups of 8!

2. What have you learned about division?

    During our division unit I learned that division is very easy. There are more than eight ways to do division. Did you know that? Some of the ways we learned are repeated addition, repeated subtraction, guess and check, multiples (the one I just showed you above) and more. Division and multiplication are just opposites.

Seventh Grade Ratio/Proportion/Percent Unit

Name _Brad_   Date _4-26-2000_

Performance Task Self-Reflection

1. Discuss how you did on the performance task for this unit. What are you pleased with? What could you have done better?

   > I did ok on my performance task. I was pleased with its organization and neatness and I was pleased that the way I chose to solve the problem worked (by diagramming where each of the runners was). I was able to explain my solution, proving that I understood the information in the focus statement. I realized the performance task let me show that I have learned the focus statements for this unit.

2. What is your specific plan for improvement? What will you do differently next time?

   > Because I kept my ongoing table of contents in order throughout the unit and completed all my assignments, I felt prepared to do well on the performance task. I plan to continue in the same way for the next unit.

8. Compile and grade the unit folder for inclusion in the math portfolio.

The math unit is now complete, and it's time to compile the unit folder. Students add the remaining items (the scoring guide, performance task, self-reflection, and a Problem-of-the-Week related to the unit focus of division—described in Chapter Three) to their table of contents. The specific number of papers to be included in the unit folder varies according to the length of the unit and the number of assignments the teacher directs the students to include.

All completed unit papers go into a construction-paper folder or index file folder sequenced according to the table of contents. Students label the cover of the folder with their name, title of the math unit, and any other identifying information required. On the inside cover, they list the four criteria that will be used by the teacher to grade the folder:

- Neat

- Complete

- On-time

- Organized

Each criterion counts for one point with "4" being the top score. The "weighting" of these four criteria is determined by the teacher and announced to the students at the beginning of the unit so they don't mistakenly conclude that neatness alone makes up for omitted assignments! Teachers need to determine for themselves what percentage of the overall math grade for any given unit the unit folder should be.

We send each student's graded unit folder home for parent review and comments before placing it into the mathematics portfolio—an ongoing collection of the year's math unit folders that is reviewed during parent conferences and at other times during the school year. We also forward representative samples of student learning to the next year's math teacher. The balance of the portfolio is given to the student at the end of the academic year.

9. Spend a few moments engaged in your own self-reflection.

With the unit now completed, the teacher reflects on the following three questions.

- What went well in the design and implementation of this unit? What didn't?

- What insights into student learning did the performance task provide me?

- What changes or improvements do I want to make in designing my next unit?

Step Two
Reader's Assignment

Begin designing your next math unit based on this Conceptual Unit model. First determine your focus statements or questions in consideration of district standards and benchmarks for the particular strand of mathematics you plan to teach next. Then select an end-of-unit performance task aligned with your unit focus. After that, follow the remaining sequence of steps provided at the beginning of this chapter. You may wish to use the Conceptual Unit Planning Template in the appendix as your design tool.

CHAPTER

3

Step 3: Problem Solving and Math Application

The problem-solving step of a balanced math program provides students with a dual opportunity:

1. To apply the mathematics they have learned in the Conceptual Unit to a problem-solving situation

2. To communicate their mathematical thinking to others

Mathematics and language processes are interrelated. Our underlying purpose in asking students to communicate their thinking in oral and written form is not to turn the math classroom into a language arts class but to teach students how to explain their process to others. In doing this, students develop the ability to think logically and follow the sequence of mental steps needed to solve math-related problems in real life.

We recognize that some students do this process automatically and are able to arrive at the answer quite quickly. But when you ask these students how they solved the problem, they frequently reply, "I just figured it out in my head." Other students are never quite sure how to approach a problem if it is not already in an arithmetic format. Because our goal is to produce mathematically powerful students who can reason, solve, and explain both procedural and application problems, we need to set up learning experiences wherein they *articulate* the mathematical process they followed— first for themselves, and then for others.

Selecting the Problem-of-the-Week

In the first stage of developing students' problem solving skills, we want to introduce students to the *process* of *mathematically* showing how to solve a complex word problem requiring more than one step. The Problem-of-the-Week provides students with the opportunity to practice this. It is a carefully selected problem matched to the unit focus statements or questions that students discuss, solve, and write about during the course of a week.

When selecting a particular problem for students to solve in order to demonstrate their application of the unit focus, we refer to these guiding questions:

- Does this problem allow for the application of the mathematical ideas presented in the current conceptual unit?

- Does this problem match students' current instructional level?

- Is this problem accessible to all students?

- Does this problem require students to "stretch" their mathematical reasoning abilities?

- Does this problem involve more than one strand of mathematics?

- Do I fully understand the mathematics in this problem so I can better facilitate student understanding of the key ideas?

Teaching Students to Solve the Problem-of-the-Week

Once we select the problem, we follow a specific instructional sequence to teach students how to mathematically solve an application problem and communicate in writing the process they used.

Introduce the Selected Problem. The teacher introduces the problem to the class and helps students see its connection to the conceptual unit focus. Working alone, with a partner, or with a cooperative group, students then attempt to solve the problem without teacher assistance using words, pictures, and numbers. They next share their solutions with the rest of the class, explaining the process they followed in an attempt to convince the class that their answer is correct and makes sense. The class and teacher then discuss the different solutions presented and determine the actual answer.

Provide students with a Problem-of-the-Week Write-up Guide. The mathematical work students have done up to this point is referred to as the Data Sheet. Because we want the students to also communicate their mathematical process in writing, we now provide them with a format for doing so. Called the Problem-of-the-Week (POW) Write-up Guide, it provides an organized structure to explain the work shown on the Data Sheet. Sample Problem Write-up

Guides used by primary, intermediate, and middle school students are shown on the following pages. Teachers can use either one of these two models or create their own POW Guides depending on the grade and ability levels of their students.

Problem-of-the-Week (POW) Guide
Primary Grades

Directions:

1. Write your name on a piece of paper.

2. Write the title of the problem.

3. Solve the problem using words, pictures, and numbers.

4. Write your answer in a sentence under your solution.

5. Now write a 5-sentence paragraph that explains step-by-step how you solved the problem.

6. Use math vocabulary.

7. Write your paragraph like this:

First I _____.

Then I _____.

Next I _____.

After that I _____.

Finally I _____.

Problem-of-the-Week (POW) Guide Intermediate Grades

Follow these directions **exactly** to receive full credit:
1. Head a piece of paper with your student number, name, date, TITLE OF POW and the words DATA SHEET in printed CAPITAL LETTERS.
2. Show **all** the work you did to solve the problem using **words**, **pictures**, and **numbers**.
3. Write a concluding sentence at the end of your data sheet that clearly states the answer to the problem.

Now take a **separate** piece of paper and follow the next set of directions:
1. Write your student number, name, date, and TITLE OF THE POW in printed CAPITAL LETTERS at the top of this paper. Copy the title of each paragraph before you write your sentences for that paragraph.
2. Use the sentence starters below to complete your write-up. Everything you write must refer to the math content, procedures you followed, and strategies you used to solve the problem. Write in cursive each section in paragraph form.

Paragraph One: **Problem Statement**

    This problem is called _____. It is about
_____. I'm supposed to find
_____.

Paragraph Two: **Work Write-up**

Explain **step-by-step** in detail everything you did to complete your data sheet and arrive at your answer. Think of it like writing a recipe for someone to follow or giving a friend exact directions to your house. **See example.**

    First I _____. Then I _____
_____. Next I _____. After
that I _____. Finally I _____.

Paragraph Three: **Answer**

    My answer is _____. I think my answer makes sense because
_____. (Verify or prove your answer by referring
to the math you did – it is not enough to write that you just checked it on the
calculator or that you checked it twice or that a friend or parent or teacher told
you so.)

Problem-of-the-Week (POW) Guide
Middle School*

1. **Problem Statement**

   Rewrite the problem in your own words so someone reading your paper could understand exactly what you were asked to do. Be sure to include the question you want to answer.

2. **Plan**

   Tell what you will do to solve the problem. Which strategy will you use? Before you begin work, make a guess at the answer to the problem.

3. **Work**

   Show ALL the work you do to <u>solve</u> the problem. Use a table, graph, picture, chart, and/or arithmetic. <u>Explain</u> in detail what you did so the reader will understand your work and how you arrived at an answer. If you had problems, tell what they were and what changes you made to help you get on the right track to solving the problem.

4. **Answer**

   Write your answer to the problem in a sentence. Could there be any other answers? Compare your answer to your guess. Tell what you learned from this problem that could help you solve other problems.

* For this POW Guide, special thanks to Mrs. Arlette Byrne, Valley Middle School, Carlsbad Unified School District, Carlsbad, CA, 1996.

Class first completes Write-up together, then in cooperative groups. We have found it important to first model for the students how to complete the Problem-of-the-Week Write-up by taking them through the process together the first time. The teacher writes on large easel-size chart paper while everyone copies this model onto their own papers, including any suggested revisions that the class agrees to. Once completed, students place their written copy into the math section of their binders to serve as a model for future Write-ups.

When the teacher introduces the next Problem-of-the-Week, students can work in pairs or small cooperative groups to complete one of the assigned sections of the POW Guide on their own. Since there are more teams than there are sections on the POW Guide, several teams of students may be creating their own version of the same section as other teams in the class. This is beneficial since different teams will describe their process differently and thus add to everyone's understanding of how the problem was solved.

Student teams first write on notebook paper their team's responses to the POW Guide prompts and then transfer that information onto easel-size chart paper or onto overhead transparency sheets.

Student teams share their completed posters with class. When the students have completed their posters or overheads, each team presents their work to the entire class. This affords the teacher the opportunity to provide further instructions as to how the Write-up is to be done and respond to student questions. This modeling is critical to the long-term understanding and success of the Problem-of-the-Week Write-up process.

Display posters in classroom to serve as examples of Write-up. Once the presentations are finished, the students display their posters around the classroom. They will later refer to these models to assist them in completing subsequent Write-ups. Students exchange new posters for existing ones each time the class completes a new Problem-of-the-Week. This maintains student interest in problem solving all year long.

Students independently complete the Problem-of-the-Week. When the teacher feels that all students have had sufficient modeling and practice in completing a Data Sheet and the corresponding Write-up based on the POW Guide, s/he introduces a new Problem-of-the-Week and asks students to complete a Data Sheet and Write-up independently. The teacher reviews the work students complete on their own to determine if further clarification and instruction is needed. Once students demonstrate that they understand and can follow the process independently, the teacher can assign the Problem-of-the-Week to be completed on their own for the duration of the school year.

A weekly schedule for completing each of the POW components will be presented in the primary, intermediate, and middle school classroom implementation chapters of Part II. Included in the following pages are sample Problem-of-the-Week Write-ups from the primary, intermediate, and middle school classrooms.

Problem-of-the-Week Write-up: Primary*

Name ___Courtney___

Bean Bag Game

- Ben got 190 points with 2 tosses.
- Kim got more points than Ben.
- Show 2 different scores Kim could get.
- Explain with pictures, numbers, and words:
    - Why you chose the numbers.
    - How you found each score.

One Score

Pictures

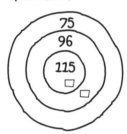

Numbers

115 + 96 = 211

Words

I just add 115
And 96 and that is
more than 190.

Another Score

Pictures

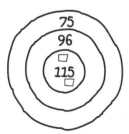

Numbers

115 + 115 = 230

Words

I took 115 and
added 115 and
that is more than
190.

How I solved this POW. First I looked at the picture of the target. Then I drew bean bags in the two highest rings of the target. Next I added those numbers together to see if they were more than Ben's score. After that I drew two beanbags in the highest ring. Finally I added 115 and 115 together and that was higher than Ben's score too.

* This POW is from the K-7 Math Performance Task Binder. For its use, special thanks to the San Diego County Office of Education and the K-2 Performance Assessment Team.

Problem-of-the-Week Write-up: Intermediate

Name ___Kelly_____ Date: _5/2/00_____

POW Data Sheet "Counting Marbles"

Find all different ways you can divide equally 144 marbles into bags.

Marbles		Bags
144 ——→	x —→	1
72 ——→	x —→	2
48 ——→	x —→	3
36 ——→	x —→	4
X		5
24 ——→	x —→	6
X		7
18 ——→	x —→	8
16 ——→	x —→	9
X		10
X		11
12 ——→	x —→	12
X		13
X		14
X		15
9 ——→	x —→	16
X		17
8 ——→	x —→	18
6	x	24
4 ——→	x —→	36
3 ——→	x —→	48
2 ——→	x —→	72
1 ——→	x —→	144

There are 15 combinations to marbles and bags.

The factors of 144 in order are

1, 2, 3, 4, 6, 8, 9, 12, 16, 18, 24, 36, 48, 72 and 144.

Problem-of-the-Week Write-up: Intermediate - Page 2

Name ___Kelly_____ Date: _5/2/00_____

POW Write-up "Counting Marbles"

Paragraph One: Problem Statements

This problem is called Counting Marbles. It is about 144 marbles in different

bags. I'm supposed to find as many combinations to make 144 equally as I can.

Paragraph Two: Work Write-up

First I took half of 144 and got 72. Then I divided 144 by 3 and got 48.

Then I did 144 ÷ 4 and got 36 because I knew half of 72 was 36. I tried to

divide 144 by 5 but it had a remainder, so I couldn't use it. After that I found

the rest of the factors that divided equally into 144. I found out that after

12x12 all the factors switched places. Finally I counted all the combinations (I

used x's in my diagram) and came up with 15.

Paragraph Three: Answer

My answer is 15. I think my answer makes sense because I made an organized

list of all the factors and combinations that equaled 144.

Problem-of-the-Week: Middle School

Name ___Tony_____   Date: _5/1/00_____

POW Data Sheet "At the Zoo"

The keeper of the bird cages at the zoo discovered that two
crested cockatoos would eat two pounds of bird seed every two
weeks; that three Peruvian parrots would eat three pounds of
bird seed every three weeks; and that four Mozambique macaws
would eat four pounds of bird seed every four weeks. How many pounds of bird
seed will 12 crested cockatoos, 12 Peruvian parrots, and 12 Mozambique macaws eat
in 12 weeks?

Tony
May 1, 2000
Period 2

Data Page: At the Zoo

CRESTED COCKATOOS:

2 birds   2 weeks

2 weeks   2 lbs x .5 = 1 lb.

2 lbs. Food

   1 bird eats 1 lb of food in two weeks, .5 lbs of food in 1 week

   .5 lb x 12 weeks = 6 lbs. Of food in 12 weeks
                    <u>x12 birds</u>
                    62 lbs. of food

PERUVIAN PARROTS:

3 birds   1 bird x 1 lb. = 3 weeks
                              <u>x4</u>
3 lbs. food   12 weeks

3 weeks

   12 ÷ 3 = 4

   1 bird = 4 lbs. food in 12 weeks

   12 birds x 4 lbs. = 48 lbs. of food in 12 weeks

MOZAMBIQUE MACAWS:

4 birds

4 lbs. food   <u>4 birds</u>
                   4 weeks = 1

   1 bird ÷ 4 lbs. = .25 lbs. per bird per week

   .25 lbs. x 12 weeks = 3 lbs. per bird

   3 lbs. x 12 birds = 36 lbs. total

TOTAL: 36 lbs.
             72 lbs.
          <u>+ 48 lbs.</u>
          156 lbs. total

The bird keeper would need to buy 156 pounds of food to feed all three groups of birds.

Tony
May 3, 2000
Period 2
Page 1 of 2

At the Zoo

1. **Problem Statement:**

   In this week's POW the bird keeper at the zoo realizes that two crested cockatoos eat two pounds of bird seed every two weeks. He also saw that three Peruvian parrots eat three pounds of bird seed every three weeks, and that four Mozambique macaws eat four pounds of bird seed for every four weeks. I'm supposed to find out how many pounds of bird seed 12 crested cockatoos, 12 Peruvian parrots, and 12 Mozambique macaws eat in 12 weeks.

2. **Plan:**

   To solve this problem I am first going to have to find out how many pounds of bird seed you would need for 12 birds of each kind. Then I'm going to have to multiply that amount of food for the 12 weeks for each kind of bird. Finally I will add all the subtotals together to get a grand total, which will tell me how much bird seed I need. After that I should have my answer. The strategies I think I will use are multiplication and division with some addition at the end. I think that you will need 72 pounds of food for the 12 crested cockatoos, 64 pounds of food for the 12 Peruvian parrots, and 56 pounds of food for the 12 Mozambique macaws, for a grand total of 192 pounds of bird seed.

3. **Work:**

   For this POW I first read the problem and started working on converting the information on the two crested cockatoos to twelve crested cockatoos, that needed food for twelve weeks. I found that 1 bird eats .5 pounds of food every two weeks. I found this by dividing 2 birds by half (.5) to get one bird, then two pounds by half to get one pound. That means that one bird eats .5 pounds of food in a week. After that I took .5 pounds of food and multiplied it by 12 weeks. This gave me the amount of food one bird would eat in 12 weeks, which is 6 pounds. Finally I took 6 pounds of food and multiplied it by the 12 birds.

   For the Peruvian parrots I converted the information on the three parrots to 12 parrots which was very similar to my approach

Tony
May 3, 2000
Period 2
Page 2 of 2

on the first step of the problem even though the basic numbers had changed. I started by dividing three birds by three pounds to get 1 bird eating 1 pound of food every three weeks. Since twelve divided by 3 is 4, I knew that 1 bird ate four pounds of food in twelve weeks. Finally I took the 12 birds and multiplied it by 4 pounds to come up with my answer, 48.

For the third part of the problem I took all the information on the 4 Mozambique macaws and converted it for the 12 macaws. I first took the 4 birds and divided it by 4 weeks to come up with 1 bird. Next I took the 1 bird and divided it by the 4 pounds and saw that 1 bird eats .25 pounds of food every week. After that I took the .25 pounds of food and multiplied it by the 12 weeks, which told me that each bird eats three pounds of food every 12 weeks. Finally I took the 3 pounds of food and multiplied it by the 12 birds, which would give me my answer of 36 for this part of the problem.

For the last part of the problem I took the subtotals from all three birds and added them together to get the final total amount of food that the bird keeper would need to buy.

4. **Answer:**
For this POW I believe that the bird keeper will need to buy 156 pounds of bird seed. 72 pounds for the cockatoos, 48 pounds for the parrots, and 36 pounds for the macaws. I do not think that there could be another answer for this problem because I found out the relationships between 1 bird and the feeding schedule from the above information and based on that answer will not change because the ratios will stay the same for each type of bird and how much and how often it was fed for 12 weeks. If the bird keeper bought any more food he would have too much and if he bought any less he would have too little. I guessed that the cockatoos would eat 72 pounds of bird seed and they did, but when I guessed that the parrots would eat 64 pounds of food I was wrong because they actually ate 48 pounds of bird food, and when I guessed that the macaws would eat 56 pounds of food I was wrong because they actually ate 36 pounds of food. From this problem I learned that it is easy to be given information, but when you have to take that information and convert it for one bird over an amount of time it can be a lot more difficult and require more steps to the solution.

Speaking from experience. It's important not to rush the process of teaching students to independently complete the Problem-of-the-Week Write-up. Doing a thorough job of initial training will prevent many future headaches for both teacher and students. While showing students how to correctly complete the first Data Sheets and Write-ups, the teacher not only teaches the correct process for students to follow but also models the use of mathematical vocabulary, clear mathematical reasoning, and verification of solution.

The goal of this training is to demonstrate for students *how* to communicate their mathematical understanding by following a specific format or structure for doing so. If teachers will spend the needed time to train their students in this process, they will see the wonderful results of their efforts in terms of students who can apply mathematical concepts and procedures to real-world situations.

Assessing Problem Solving

The first few Problems-of-the-Week are done primarily to give students the experience of solving them and becoming familiar with the format for communicating their process and understanding. We review their initial work only for completion and following directions. However, when students have successfully completed several Problem-of-the-Week Write-ups with their classmates and independently, it is time to involve them in the assessment of their work. Assessing problem solving involves three phases:

1. Creating one student-generated rubric that can be used to assess *all* Problems-of-the-Week

2. "Anchoring" students to that same rubric

3. Peer-, self-, and teacher-evaluation using the POW rubric

Creating a Student-Generated Rubric

A rubric or scoring guide is a set of performance criteria that enables both teachers and students to know the level of proficiency reached on a particular piece of student work. We believe that all rubrics need clearly understood, specific language descriptors that everyone can agree on, and that teachers need to author rubrics *with* students to be truly usable by students. Many district and state assessments now include rubrics to evaluate math tasks, but the criteria in them are highly subjective, such as the following example:

Please note the subjective terminology underlined in the math rubric above. Teachers attempting to score student papers using this rubric might find it challenging to agree with each other as to exactly what the underlined terms such as "substantially," "in large part," and "partial but limited," etc. mean. How much more difficult would it be for *students* to use this same rubric to peer-and self-assess the Problem-of-the-Week Write-ups with reliability?

The student-generated rubric for mathematical problem solving is a special type of rubric. It is *not* specific to one problem only, but must be thoughtfully written so that it can be used for *every* Problem-of-the-Week assigned.

Because it requires a sizeable block of instructional time to involve students in designing and revising assessment criteria, it is impractical to create a task-specific rubric for *each* Problem-of-the-Week. In addition, teachers run the risk of "over-rubricizing"—a term we coined to mean having students create too many rubrics and thus negating their enthusiasm for designing assessment criteria.

Problem solving rubrics need to evaluate differing content and quality. Our goal here is to create a *more generalized, yet still specific* student-generated rubric that describes the essential criteria needed to assess a Problem-of-the-Week Write-up fairly and reliably, but also one that can be used week after week.

How to Build the Problem-of-the-Week Rubric

This is the sequence we follow with our own students each school year when it's time to begin assessing the Problem-of-the-Week. Although we described in the previous chapter the process of involving students in generating a rubric to assess their end-of-unit performance task, we thought it beneficial to include the special considerations for rubric writing as they relate to the Problem-of-the-Week.

Keep it simple: Although an example of a four-level, primary grade POW Rubric is included below, we recommend using only three performance levels (1, 2, 3 or A, B, C, etc.) in primary grade classrooms. Four grading levels are more appropriate in intermediate and middle school grades. Even though five- and six-point rubrics are used in many school districts, our experience is that they are more difficult to design and use with students because the difference in descriptors between the performance levels is either too vague or too subtle for students to understand and use reliably. When students are included in scoring guide criteria design, they can suggest content and quality descriptors more easily when there are only three or four levels.

As mentioned in Chapter Two, primary grades typically use a three-number system, but these grading levels can also be three different colors, three different symbols (star, happy face, or straight face), etc. Intermediate grades typically use numbers or letter grades, so they already have an understanding of what those letter or number grades mean. We recommend using whatever grading symbols students are used to.

Refer to POW Guide and Practice Problems to Create Rubric Criteria. When students begin authoring the rubric, they look to the POW Guide and the practice problems displayed around the room to help them think of the criteria to include in the rubric. The POW Guide focuses their attention on the important issue of following Write-up directions. The posters provide powerful examples of mathematical reasoning, the use of math vocabulary, the process the students went through to arrive at the solution, and to what degree the written work communicated mathematical understanding.

Build Rubric From "Proficient," "Bottom-Up," or "Top-Down." As we pointed out in Chapter Two, many teachers and students like to begin designing rubrics by looking closely at the task requirements needed to achieve the "proficient" grade and then establishing "advanced" and "progressing" criteria from there. A few prefer to build their student-generated rubric from the bottom level to the top. Still others choose the subtractive method—starting at the top and working their way down, omitting quality and content as they go. As always, choose the approach that best matches your personal preference.

Consider the Problem-of-the-Week Rubric Issues. The following list of issues will help teachers first think through what they want the Problem-of-the-Week Rubric to evaluate before they begin creating it with their students. As you consider each issue, decide where you would place it in the performance levels you are using. This is an excellent activity to do in grade level or department teams.

- Right Answer

- Right Answer, Wrong Process

- Wrong Answer, Right Process

- Following POW Guide Directions

- Simple Calculation Errors

- Inclusion of Math Vocabulary

- Correct Sentence Format

- Spelling and Mechanics

Involving All Students. When beginning rubric writing, we try to involve the entire class as much as possible while soliciting student suggestions and recording those suggestions on large chart paper. However, our experience is that a few students invariably volunteer all the ideas while the others remain passive observers. Because our goal is to actively involve everyone, we change our approach once the class is familiar with the procedure for recording rubric ideas on paper.

Students Work In Cooperative Teams. We ask each student to independently record his or her own ideas for each performance level. This can be done in class or assigned for homework. When this is completed, we direct the students to combine their ideas with the ideas of three or four other students sitting near them, or with their cooperative group team, and produce a "team" rubric that is a compilation of their best ideas.

Combine Ideas From Four Teams Into One Rubric. In a classroom of 32 students, there will be approximately eight team rubrics. So we next ask the eight teams to each choose one representative who will take the team rubric and meet with the representatives of three other teams. The representatives from four teams gather together in one corner of the classroom, and the representatives from the other four teams meet in another. Their job is to now combine the rubrics from four teams into one.

Combine Two "Semi-Finalist" Rubrics Into "Finalist" Rubric. These two groups will now create two "semi-finalist" rubrics, each representing the combined thinking of four teams. These two rubrics are then combined into one "finalist" rubric that reflects the suggestions from the entire class. Once this is accomplished, the teacher makes an overhead transparency of the "finalist" rubric and conducts a final revision and editing session with all the students. The student-generated Problem-of-the-Week Rubric is then typed and distributed to everyone for use throughout the remainder of the year.

An alternative method for middle school teachers to consider is to have first period math students create the initial draft of the Problem-of-the-Week Rubric, and then ask second period students to add their suggestions, followed by third period, etc. In this way, all students who will eventually use the Problem-of-the-Week Rubric can provide input even though they cannot all be together in the same classroom at the same time.

The following pages feature three Problem-of-the-Week Rubric examples from the primary, intermediate, and middle school math classrooms that were generated by teachers and students working together. Please note that certain criteria may seem subjective to the reader. We are not including these rubrics to stand as "perfect" examples, but rather as models to help teachers and students begin the process of creating their own.

Name _____ Title of Problem _____

Problem-of-the-Week PRIMARY Grade Math Rubric

4

- All "3" Criteria
- Includes Extra Work:
  - Uses Words, Pictures, **and** Numbers
  - Paragraph Includes Extra Math Steps Taken to Solve Problem
  - Paragraph Explains Why Answer Is Correct
  - May Show Other Ways to Solve Problem

3

- Correct Answer
- All POW Guide Directions Followed:
  - Write Student name
  - Write Title Of Problem
  - Solve Problem Using Words with Pictures **OR** Numbers
  - Write Answer In Sentence Under Solution
  - Use Math Vocabulary
  - Write 5-Sentence Paragraph That Explains Step-By-Step How Problem Was Solved

2

- Incorrect Answer or
- Correct Answer, But Math Doesn't Show How Problem Was Solved
  Something is Missing:
  - Didn't Write Student Name
  - Didn't Write Title Of Problem
  - Didn't Solve Problem Using Words with Pictures **or** Numbers
  - Didn't Write Answer In Sentence Under Solution
  - 5-Sentence Paragraph Doesn't Explain Step-By-Step How Problem Was Solved

1

- Incorrect Answer
- Missing Two or More Parts of the Directions

Self-Grade _____
I think my grade is a _____ because_____
_____

Teacher's Grade _____ because_____
_____

Problem-of-the-Week INTERMEDIATE Grade Math Rubric

4
- All "3" Criteria
- Advanced Work is Evident:
  — Data Sheet Includes Words, Pictures, **and** Numbers
  — No Calculation Errors
  — Paragraph Two Contains Math Vocabulary That Adds to Understanding of Process Followed
  — Paragraph Three Includes Correct or Detailed Justification
  — May Show Other Ways to Solve Problem
  — 0-2 Spelling and Mechanics Errors Total

3
- Correct Answer
- Follows POW Guide **Completely**:
  — Data Sheet Includes Numbers with Words **or** Pictures
  — Data Sheet Process Followed is Correct and Makes Sense
  — No Calculation Errors or Errors That Don't Produce Wrong Answer
  — Data Sheet Includes Answer Written in Sentence
  — Paragraph One Includes All Information Needed to Solve Problem
  — Paragraph Two Includes **Specific** Math Steps Used to Solve Problem
  — Paragraph Two Includes Math Vocabulary
  — Paragraph Three Includes Correct Answer **and** A Justification
  — Correct Sentence Format in All Three Paragraphs
  — 3-5 Spelling and Mechanics Errors Total

2
- Incorrect Answer or
- Correct Answer, But Process Followed Incomplete, Doens't Make Sense
  Doesn't Follow POW Guide Completely
  — Data Sheet Contains Calculation Errors That Produce Wrong Answer
  — Data Sheet May Be Missing Answer Written in Sentence
  — Paragraph One May Be Missing Information Needed to Solve Problem
  — Paragraph Two May Be Missing Specific Math Steps
  — Paragraph Two May Be Missing Math Vocabulary
  — Paragraph Three May Be Missing Justification
  — May Include Incorrect Sentence Format
  — More than 5 Spelling and Mechanics Errors Total

1
- Incorrect Answer
- Missing One or More Sections Required on POW Guide
  — More Work Needed

Peer-Graders _____ and _____ **Grade** _____
Justification _____

Self-Grade _____ Justification _____

_____

Teacher's Grade _____ Justification _____

_____

Name _____ Date _____

Period _____ Title of Problem _____

Problem-of-the-Week MIDDLE SCHOOL Math Rubric

A

- Correct Answer
- Explanation matches data sheet
- Clear mathematical reasoning
- Explanation uses math vocabulary
- All "Write-up Guide" requirements complete

B

- Correct answer
- Explanation matches data sheet
- Clear mathematical reasoning
- Explanation uses math vocabulary
- 1-2 items missing from "Write-up Guide"

C

- Correct or incorrect answer
- Explanation does not match data sheet
- Mathematical reasoning unclear
- Math vocabulary missing
- 2-4 items missing from "Write-up Guide"

D

- Incorrect answer
- 1 or more sections from "Write-up Guide" missing
- Data sheet missing
- More than 4 items missing from "Write-up Guide"

Using the Rubric to Assess

"Anchoring" the Students to the Rubric. After creating, revising, and publishing the Problem-of-the-Week Rubric for all to use, the teacher shows the students how to use the rubric by means of an "anchoring" process that enables them to evaluate reliably the work of their peers and then their own. This procedure was introduced in Chapter Two but is expanded here to include the writing of comments related to the rubric criteria during the peer-grading process.

The teacher collects the students' completed Problem Write-ups and selects several papers representative of different performance levels to read to the class. The teacher and students review the rubric so that the criteria for each performance level are fresh in their minds. The teacher makes certain everyone knows the correct answer to the problem and then reads the first anonymous sample paper. The students identify the presence or absence of rubric criteria. Students and teacher together discuss what the grade should be, based on the rubric criteria.

Modeling the writing of appropriate grading comments. The purpose of the written comments is to provide individual students with specific feedback as to which rubric criteria were successfully met and those that were omitted or need improvement. The teacher models the writing of appropriate (i.e. related to rubric criteria) comments on a student's paper and then repeats the same process with another student's paper. After reading a third paper aloud, the teacher encourages students to practice writing appropriate feedback remarks for that paper similar to the way s/he modeled it with the previous two. It's important to read enough sample papers so that students become familiar with a wide range of student responses. This better enables them to assess accurately any paper they are given and to write constructive feedback on any paper they assess.

Partnering Students. When the teacher feels the students are sufficiently trained to assess the work of their peers using the class-generated rubric, s/he assigns each student a grading partner. By making this partnering decision rather than allowing students to choose their own, the teacher can match students of differing abilities, second-language learners with English speakers, special education students with regular education students, and so forth.

We recommend not having primary students peer-assess, but to self-assess only. As stated before, this is not a hard and fast rule, but one that depends on the maturity of the individual class. Many primary students are not quite ready to assess the work of their peers, but primary teachers can lay the foundation for peer-assessment before their students reach the intermediate grades by teaching students to determine accurately whether they followed directions on their own work.

Upper elementary and middle school students can peer-assess effectively, given clear guidelines and adequate training. But we have also found that middle school students may do better grading another student's paper by themselves, rather than with a partner. The paper can then be passed to another individual student to assess, thus giving the paper a second grading and validation that it was correctly assessed according to the Problem-of-the-Week Rubric.

Peer-grading & Paper-flow Procedures. The assigned grading partners (or individual students) receive their first paper to assess from the teacher, or the teacher may direct them to take one from the "ungraded" pile. We instruct students not to score their own or their scoring partner's paper. The scoring partners record their names on the owner's rubric, then read through the entire paper to get an overall sense of the content. After this, they reread the paper and place a check on the rubric next to each criterion they identify. We give each grading partnership a yellow highlighter and instruct them to highlight any criterion they believe is missing. Students may start with the top grade category and work their way down, or begin with the lowest grade category and work their way up. They determine the grade by finding *the highest category with all criteria checked.*

Once the grade is determined, student partners write appropriate feedback comments on the owner's paper. We remind them to base their comments on the rubric. When finished, they bring the scored paper to the teacher for a quick review to make sure it was done correctly. If the paper is acceptable, the teacher directs them to place it in the "graded" pile and take the next paper from the "ungraded" pile. If the paper has not been assessed correctly, the teacher sends the partners back with suggestions on how to revise their grade and/or comments. The process continues until all papers have been peer-assessed.

Nominating "Great" Papers. We invite peer-graders who come across an exemplary paper during grading to write the owner's name on the board. After all the papers have been peer-assessed, the teacher or students can read the paper aloud and invite the class to share thoughts as to why the explanation is especially good. This benefits all students by providing them with "anchor paper" examples of well-written mathematical explanations. Students can then think about how to improve their own problem-solving work in the future based on the examples of nominated papers.

Self-Grading. When all the papers have been peer-assessed, the teacher returns them to their owners for self-assessment. At this point, students who believe their paper to be unfairly graded may "appeal" their grade to the teacher. But this appeal must be in writing, and it must relate to the rubric criteria. It's not enough to cry, "But I worked so hard on this, and my mom even said it's right." The rubric provides the fairness and objectivity to assess all papers reliably.

It is left to the teacher's discretion whether to allow students to make further revisions to receive a higher grade. Often only one or two minor changes are needed. Being given the opportunity to revise work based on the peer-graders' feedback can provide the student with a powerful motivation to improve. Such opportunities can result in students becoming more interested in closely following directions and doing more careful editing and revising of work on future Problems-of-the-Week.

The Final Grade. The teacher now collects the peer-assessed and self-assessed papers, reviews both grades and related student comments, and determines the final grade. The papers with attached rubrics and final grades are then returned to the students. Teachers may require parent review of the Problem-of-the-Week before including it in the current Conceptual Unit folder. Students are now ready for the next Problem-of-the-Week, either later in the current Conceptual Unit or in the unit to follow.

Benefits of the Problem-of-the-Week

Teachers who make the Problem-of-the-Week a regular part of their balanced math program will see firsthand its many benefits. Students who consistently and regularly engage in structured problem-solving activities will find themselves better prepared to reason mathematically and to think logically. They will be able to apply their problem-solving skills successfully, not only in the math classroom and on standardized test measures, but also in the authentic math situations they are sure to encounter throughout life.

Step Three
Reader's Assignment

Begin designing the Problem Solving component for your planned math unit based on the information presented in this chapter. First select a problem aligned to your Conceptual Unit's focus statements or questions. Then decide if the suggested sequence for training students in the process of problem solving, rubric writing, and assessment will work for you and your students. Make whatever modifications are necessary. Refer to the grade-specific problem solving references in Chapters Six, Seven, and Eight.

CHAPTER

4

Step 4: Mastery of Basic Facts

Just as learning to count is a prerequisite skill that very young children need before they can begin exploring and manipulating number concepts, mastery of basic number facts is a necessary building block for students as they move up through the first formal years of schooling. By the time students leave elementary school, they should have these facts firmly committed to memory. Yet many middle school teachers report this is not the case. The fourth step in our balanced math program suggests ways elementary teachers can help their students master basic math facts *before* they enter middle school.

Students who do not learn their math facts find this an impediment to solving problems accurately and in an appropriate amount of time. This leads to frustration and weakens their perception of themselves as mathematically powerful students, the self-concept we as educators strive so diligently to promote—in our unit planning, our engaging lessons and activities, and our methods of assessment.

Marilyn Burns has this to say with regard to students learning their basic number facts: "Memorization plays an important role in computation. Calculating mentally or with paper and pencil requires having basic number facts committed to memory. However, memorization should follow, not lead, instruction that builds children's understanding. The emphasis of learning in mathematics must always be on thinking, reasoning, and making sense" (1999).

How, then, do we help students master the necessary skill of math fact recall?

Emphasizing Patterns

We have found that helping students discover patterns makes it easier and more interesting to memorize number facts. Therefore, we strive to create a classroom environment that emphasizes patterns, presents number facts in a way that makes sense, and reinforces fact acquisition through regular practice.

We present lessons that demonstrate the various patterns in our number system. One method for doing this is to teach children the addition and subtraction "fact families:"

$$5 + 3 = 8$$
$$3 + 5 = 8$$
$$8 - 3 = 5$$
$$8 - 5 = 3$$

and the multiplication and division "fact families:"

$$2 \times 3 = 6$$
$$3 \times 2 = 6$$
$$6 \div 3 = 2$$
$$6 \div 2 = 3$$

Fact families help students recognize the unique relationships between the mathematical operations of addition and subtraction, multiplication and division.

Another method to help children learn their multiplication facts is to teach them all the factors and factor combinations of a given number. By asking students to find all the ways to make 12 in multiplication (1 x 12, 2 x 6, 3 x 4), the teacher is also creating the perfect opportunity to introduce the concept of prime and composite numbers.

Discovering the patterns within products of multiplication facts is also helpful for children striving to learn their math facts. When students see that the products of all the fives, for example, can be found by skip-counting specific intervals of that number again and again, the stage is set for introducing students to the concept of multiples. Further examples of using patterns to help students learn their multiplication facts appear later in this chapter.

Determine Grade-Appropriate Facts

To determine when children should master their addition, subtraction, multiplication, and division facts, start by consulting district and state mathematics standards and discussing grade level expectations with colleagues. It is helpful to agree upon this at the individual school site. When teachers decide together which facts need to be learned in first grade, second grade, and so on, and then communicate these expectations to parents, the cumulative result at the end of elementary school is a body of students who know their facts!

Typically, first grade students work with addition facts to ten or higher. Second graders learn addition and subtraction facts up to 20. Third graders continue practicing addition and subtraction facts and begin learning easier multiplication facts (twos, threes, fours, fives, nines, and tens). They discover the relationship between addition and multiplication (repeated addition, such as $3 + 3 + 3$ representing three groups of three or $3 \times 3 = 9$). Fourth graders practice and attempt to master the remaining multiplication facts and the corresponding division facts.

We believe that fifth grade is the year students need to demonstrate that they have mastered the number facts in all four basic operations. Fifth graders are on the verge of entering middle school or junior high school mathematics classes where such prior learning is expected. Therefore we hold them to a more rigorous accountability than we do younger children. We notify fifth grade parents of the results of each assessment and require those students not demonstrating mastery to do extra practice nightly until mastery is achieved and verified through subsequent re-testing.

Inform Parents at Beginning of Year

Parents play a major role in helping their children memorize basic math facts. Parents understand the importance of memorizing math facts because they once had to learn them, too! Students know their math facts need to be memorized. Teachers tell them so every year. Yet not all students motivate themselves to commit them to memory. Parent support and assistance are therefore essential, and it is up to the teacher to communicate the need for that support and establish a program of accountability to ensure it.

Traditional events at the beginning of the school year such as Back-to-School Night and the teacher's welcome letter provide excellent opportunities to inform parents of the specific number facts their children will need to learn that year.

Most of the pressure for memorizing facts does come in the upper elementary years, when students must demonstrate mastery of multiplication facts. We came across the following "Multiplication Facts Made Easy" chart. Being able to show fourth and fifth grade students and parents that only a handful of multiplication facts require actual memorization is encouraging news for all. Although we are unable to attribute this chart to its unknown author, we include it here in hopes that it will help lighten the load of math facts memorization for students everywhere.

Multiplication Facts Made Easy

	1	2	3	4	5	6	7	8	9	10
1	1									
2	1	❑								
3	1	Dbl	❑							
4	1	Dbl	3x4	❑						
5	1	Dbl	V	V	❑					
6	1	Dbl	3x6	4x6	V	❑				
7	1	Dbl	3x7	4x7	V	6x7	❑			
8	1	Dbl	3x8	4x8	V	6x8	7x8	❑		
9	1	Dbl	3x9	4x9	V	6x9	7x9	8x9	❑	
10	X	X	X	X	X	X	X	X	X	X

Reducing 100 Facts to 15 (plus some special projects)

1. Introduce Multiplication: Use number blocks, arrays, etc.
   Define terms (repeated addition of equal groups)

2. Teach the short table (1's to 3's):
   1x1 through 3x3; almost any student can learn these.

3. Teach 1x (1): One times the number equals the number.

4. Teach 10x (X): Ten times a number equals the number and a zero.

5. Teach 2x (Dbl): Two times a number (Double the number).

6. Teach 5x: (V): Five times a number (think of a clock).

7. Teach Squares (❑): The number times itself.

8. Teach the 15 remaining facts.

9. Teach Commutivity: Commutative Law states that 3x5 and 5x3 have the same product (for the unmarked areas above).

Establish Timeline to Assess Progress

At the beginning of a school year, we allow two or three months of practice without assessment before holding the students accountable by means of testing. After that, we establish a regular testing schedule that will be described below.

It is important to let parents know how often students will be tested for fact memorization. Our experience has been that with a regular system of accountability—a weekly or biweekly quiz, for example—there's a much greater likelihood that students and parents will make the memorization of facts a priority.

Assess What Students Presently Know

In beginning your program to promote math fact mastery, first assess what students currently know by using a timed, written test or by administering individual verbal tests. Then systematically plan into the math program regular opportunities for children to practice facts in as non-threatening a climate as possible. As described below, the Math Review and Mental Math portions of the daily math period provide excellent practice opportunities for students.

In both primary and upper elementary grades, teachers generally use their own self-made or commercially produced quizzes. Whatever the format used, whether that same format is used in only one classroom or across several grade levels within a school, the important consideration is, once again, its consistent use.

Provide Daily Practice Materials

The key to unlocking student success with math facts prior to formal testing is regular, systematic practice, both in school and at home. Here are several suggestions for helping elementary students memorize their number facts at home and in school:

- Orally practice all the twos, threes, fours, etc. with a family member, classmate, or teacher aide—first by groupings, then at random, and finally with all the facts mixed together

- Flash card practice all the twos, threes, fours, etc. with a family member, classmate, or teacher aide —by groupings, then at random, then all together

- Notice product *patterns* for multiplication:

    - Look at product patterns for five (0, 5, 10, 15, 20, 25, 30, 35, 40, 45) where the ones digit alternates between zero and five

- Look at product patterns of three (3, 6, 9 where 3 + 6 = 9) and the remaining products (12, 15, 18, 21, 24, 27) where the sum of the two digits equals three, six, or nine

- Look at product patterns of nine (9, 18, 27, 36, 45, 54, 63, 72, 81) where the sum of the two digits equals nine, the tens digits are sequenced in order from one to nine and the ones digits are sequenced in reverse, from nine to one

• Count aloud the multiples of a given number

• Learn the "Fact Families" in addition, subtraction, multiplication, and division

• Write math facts each day in school and at home

• Play math facts games and utilize computer software math facts programs

• Use practice worksheets

Math Review & Mental Math

Math Review and Mental Math also provide excellent opportunities for students to practice and learn their basic number facts when solving procedural math problems or mentally calculating a sequence of numbers and operations. Students must recall number facts from memory or search them out from an external source (i.e. asking their teacher or another student, consulting a number facts chart, using their fingers, or working it out on paper). The more adept students become at math fact recall, the easier it is for them to solve the given problems correctly and quickly.

A Simple Management System

Administering the math facts assessment regularly can be a daunting task, especially if the teacher has to score all the papers, keep track of which students s/he needs to retest, and schedule re-tests and make-ups for absent students. We have used the following system with excellent results.

We set up an expanding file system, like Pendaflex, and label the different folders according to the specific facts. For example, in multiplication, the first folder is labeled "0 – 2 Cumulative Quiz", the second is labeled 3's, then the 0 – 3 Cumulative Quiz, then the 4's and 0 – 4 Cumulative Quiz, and so on through the 12's. We keep the files stocked with enough copies, both for the initial test, practice papers for homework, and subsequent re-tests. Students learn how to go to the files and select the particular quiz they need. We organize the file system for division facts in the same manner.

Helping Students Handle Time Pressure

Most students like the challenge of writing the sum, difference, product, or quotient under a respective addition, subtraction, multiplication, or division fact. But ask students to perform within a limited time, and that enjoyment remains high for those who love challenges, but it plummets drastically for those who don't. All the rationale in the world about why these quizzes must be timed proves ineffective when students are trying their best to perform but just can't get those answers on the paper fast enough.

How fast should students be expected to perform accurately on a math facts quiz? This is an issue to be decided by individual teachers, grade levels, or the entire school. Caring as teachers do about promoting positive self-esteem in the mathematics classroom, it seems counterproductive to apply a time constraint to the administration of a quiz, knowing the effect it will have on certain students.

So why do it? If the goal for these quizzes is prompt and correct math fact recall as a prerequisite skill for solving math problems of all kinds in any kind of timed context, it is necessary to require that they do so at some point in their schooling. Teachers must consider the unique needs of their own students and then decide among themselves how best to introduce the timed aspect of the math facts quiz.

When It's Time to Start Testing

The first week you plan to quiz, distribute a letter on Monday to inform parents that your math facts accountability program is beginning. Give each student a copy of the number facts you have selected to test. Tell the class they will use this paper to practice during the coming week, and that on Friday, you will give them a clean copy of the same paper, or a different sequence of the same problems that they've studied, to be completed without help in the pre-determined amount of time. Let them know how much time they will have and practice once or twice together so they can experience the time factor prior to the actual test.

Urge students to practice at home with their parents every night and to use word and number associations or other creative ways to remember the facts that are difficult for them. Remind them of the patterns they have learned. Remind them also that they have practiced these facts in fun ways at school and at home, and that many of these facts they already know. Encourage them to take a practice quiz at home within the predetermined time limit so they are again simulating the testing conditions. Announce your criteria for passing the quiz. Throughout the week and even before the quiz on Friday, orally review the facts you will be testing.

Quiz Day

Distribute a copy of the quiz to each student. Direct students to write their names on their papers, turn their papers over, and wait for the "go" signal. Students often enjoy the synchronized "swish" sound when the entire class turns over its papers at once and begins. Mark time in minutes, writing the elapsed time on the board for anyone who wants to see. We do not call out the times because this seems to put extra stress on many students.

When there are only 30 seconds remaining, we direct students to stop, hold their pencils in the air, look down at their papers, and determine how many more facts they need to do. We then announce that 30 seconds remain and encourage students to write as many more answers in the time remaining as they can. This seems to help focus students and prepare their minds for the impending "time's up" announcement.

Grading, Collecting, Recording Scores

The following grading practice may not be appropriate for lower primary students, but upper primary, intermediate, and even middle school students can certainly carry out this procedure effectively.

At the conclusion of the allotted testing time, direct students to exchange papers. Instruct students to mark the papers according to your directions as you both say the answers aloud and write them on an overhead transparency of the actual quiz.

Collect only the papers that meet the passing criteria you established with students, and instruct the rest of the students to keep their papers and continue practicing for the re-test. Record in your gradebook only those students who passed this particular quiz.

Once you begin quizzing the students on their math facts, continue this procedure weekly or biweekly so students regard it as an ongoing, regular part of your balanced math program. These quizzes will allow students and parents to gauge progress toward the end goal of mastering *all* the grade level facts.

Periodically test students who have already demonstrated mastery to make sure they still know their facts. Holding students accountable for fact mastery throughout the school year is a safeguard for long-term fact retention.

Extra Practice Required

We notify parents of students who do not show an acceptable level of mastery on a particular quiz and require additional daily practice from those students. We often ask parent volunteers in the classroom to assist us with math facts record keeping, organizing additional practice papers to go home with those students who must do extra practice, and working with students who are struggling.

Re-testing

We suggest three approaches to re-testing. The first is to re-test the student on the same facts the following week while those who *did* pass take the next quiz in the sequence. This focuses each student's attention on mastering one set of facts before moving on to the next.

The second approach is to allow the student to re-test during the coming week and take the next test in the sequence along with the rest of the class the following Friday. This works well for students who want to keep pace with their classmates, but it may put too much pressure on those having difficulty remembering their facts.

The third way is to take the entire class through the sequence of facts you expect them to learn that year and then go back and re-test students on the quizzes they have yet to master. This approach often works best because it provides ongoing review of all the facts and prevents low-performing students from feeling that they are behind the rest of the class.

Summing Up

It *is* possible to help all students achieve mastery of their basic number facts. Teachers who have been the most successful in producing students who can recall their facts follow this proven three-part formula:

1. Teach math facts in the context of patterns.

2. Provide ongoing practice in and out of the classroom.

3. Establish a regular timeline for accountability testing, inform parents, and enlist their support.

Step Four
Reader's Assignment

Plan how you will incorporate math facts into your balanced math program.

1. Determine the grade-appropriate facts you want your students to master.

2. Consider how you will teach math facts through patterns.

3. Establish your timeline to regularly assess student progress and draft your parent letter.

4. Select your math facts assessment program and gather necessary instructional and practice materials.

5. Reflect on the other suggestions we have included in this chapter to help you ready this component of your balanced math program.

CHAPTER

5

Step Five: The "Big Idea" Performance Task

In the book's Introduction, we presented the concept of the "Big Idea," identifying one number strand focus at each grade level and teaching it thoroughly so as to better prepare elementary students for middle school mathematics. We identified sample number strand "Big Ideas" for grades kindergarten through seven.

Math experts and research organizations throughout the world have validated this concept of identifying and teaching *in depth* a grade level math focus.

The Third International Mathematics and Science Study (TIMSS) 1994-95 finds:

> Currently, U.S. standards are unfocused and aimed at the lowest common denominator. In other words, they are a mile wide and an inch deep...
>
> Some countries performing better than the U.S. cover sometimes half as many topics as we do in a given year, and topics remain in the curricula for shorter periods of time, giving the impression that a more focused curriculum may lead to higher achievement.
>
> In keeping with the incremental 'assembly line' philosophy in American society, U.S. teachers also tend to lean toward a piecemeal approach to education. The results of the TIMSS achievement study... show that U.S. students do not fare well with a system dominated by such a splintered vision" (Report #7, p. 12).

The study also reported that out of the 41 countries participating, in eighth grade performance comparisons the United States ranked 28th in math and 17th in science. Yet in fourth grade, the U.S. ranked in 2nd place. What accounts for the dramatic fall in U.S. math performance between grades four and eight?

One prominent set of statistics may point to the answer. In the U.S., the average number of math topics "covered" in one year is 78. By contrast, Japan only targets 17 and Germany 23. The percentage of "high rigor" topics (those requiring students to solve complex, multi-step problems) in Japan is 30%, whereas in the U.S. it is 0%.

The TIMSS also found that in the U.S, the instructional format for the mathematics classroom is as follows: the teacher instructs and often solves the problem, then has the students practice what s/he has just demonstrated. In Japan, however, the teacher poses a complex problem, and the students struggle to solve it. The students then present their solutions, and the class debates alternative solutions. The teacher's role is to summarize the solutions offered by the students and to provide them with further practice in solving similar types of problems.

Our reason for citing this study is not to extol the mathematics teaching practices of other countries over the United States, but to point out the logic in teaching for depth of understanding versus covering superficially more topics than students can possibly understand and retain within the course of one school year.

The Big Idea Vision

When we developed the Big Idea in Carlsbad, California, we never intended it to be the only math concept within the number strand that elementary teachers would instruct during the school year, but the one *for which they would assume responsibility*. Students certainly needed to learn other important concepts in several strands within the course of one school year, yet we knew the folly of trying to cover *every* concept in the grade level math book. We embraced the idea of teaching "an inch wide and a mile deep."

Middle school teachers were eager to engage students in more advanced and challenging mathematics. We reasoned that if all elementary math teachers within the district agreed to teach their grade level Big Idea for depth of understanding, and to then assess it with a district-wide performance task, student learning within all schools would become more equitable and all students would enter middle school ready for middle school math.

The Big Idea Performance Task quickly emerged as Step Five of our balanced math program.

The Grade Level "Big Ideas"

Each grade's Big Idea laid the number strand foundation for the grade that followed it. At kindergarten, the focus was on children acquiring number sense. In first grade, teachers would reinforce number sense by expanding it to include addition. In second grade, students would continue addition, but target subtraction as the number strand focus. The goal for third graders was to understand the concept of multiplication completely. Fourth grade would build on multiplication but develop conceptual understanding of division. In fifth grade, students would learn fractions in depth.

The middle school not only recognized the worth of this plan for elementary students but also saw its applicability for their own students. The relationship between fractions, decimals, and percentages became the Big Idea for sixth grade. Seventh grade identified their Big Idea as ratio, proportion, and percent. Eighth grade chose not to focus on the number strand, but elected instead to target concepts within the algebra strand.

The Big Idea Performance Task

The purpose of having students complete an on-demand performance task aligned to a designated grade-level focus was to have a valid and reliable measure of their Big Idea understanding. A well-developed performance task would also help each teacher evaluate the effectiveness of his or her related classroom instruction and make changes where needed.

In the spring of each year, the Big Idea Performance Task was given to all K-7 students and scored by grade-level teams of teachers using rubrics they had created specific to each task. Student scores were used at the school and district level to gauge the effectiveness of instructional lessons and activities and to plan for improvements in the process for the subsequent school year. Elementary teachers throughout the district reported noticeable progress in student achievement of foundational math skills from year to year. Middle School teachers saw the math "learning gap" for all incoming students beginning to narrow.

The Implementation Sequence

To implement the Big Idea vision, the district math committee members, working collaboratively with district administrators, organized their efforts around the following sequence of tasks. We present this sequence here as a roadmap for other schools or districts interested in beginning a similar "Big Idea" journey.

- Identify the number strand Big Idea for each grade level and correlate each one with preceding and succeeding grades

- Review state and district mathematics standards to see if the proposed Big Ideas for each grade level reflect the same emphasis

- Present the Big Ideas to plan to district administrators, site principals, and elementary math teacher representatives to solicit discussion, clarification, revision, and support

- Meet in grade level teams to identify conceptual lessons to address each grade's Big Idea in the district-adopted math program or in supplemental resource materials

- Review all available resource materials and select or design one or more grade level performance tasks to assess each grade's Big Idea

- Create, in grade level teams, a task-specific rubric or scoring guide to assess levels of student performance on planned performance tasks

- Field-test the performance tasks at each grade level

- Assess, in grade level teams, the field-tested student performance tasks using the scoring guide created by the grade level team

- Select student work to serve as exemplars or "anchor papers" for each performance level at each grade

- Schedule and conduct district-wide staff development training for each grade level using recommended instructional materials, selected performance tasks, team-generated rubrics, and student anchor papers

- Provide site support where needed as all elementary math teachers implement the program

- Develop, field test, and revise grade-specific practice performance tasks similar in format and difficulty to the final Big Idea performance tasks

- Administer final grade-level performance tasks near end of school year

- Evaluate, in grade-level teams, all student-completed performance tasks district-wide at each grade level using the rubric specifically created to assess them

- Utilize results as one of several measures to show student progress within each school, grade level, and district

Benefits for Everyone

The Big Idea performance task program can greatly benefit individual schools as well as the entire district. It supports standards-based education and sets consistent performance standards to be met within each individual classroom, grade level, school, and district. It provides valuable information regarding effectiveness of instruction and students' ability to communicate their mathematical understanding. The Big Idea performance task serves as a multiple measure assessment tool for gauging overall student math achievement. Equally important, it provides teachers with valuable training in performance assessment and the evaluation of student performance using a task-specific scoring guide.

Utilizing the Big Idea in Individual Schools or Grade Levels

This process need not be implemented district-wide in order to prove effective. An individual school or grade can utilize the same process and receive powerful math assessment feedback. The communication that takes place between grade-level teachers when developing Big Idea performance tasks and rubrics and then collectively evaluating student work is vitally important. Grade-level or math department teachers discuss and ultimately reach consensus of what constitutes proficient student work, a process that eventually extends to a larger math vision for the school and finally to the district as a whole. The Big Idea sharpens instructional focus, aligns instruction with assessment, and deepens student understanding and application of grade-specific key mathematical concepts.

The Individual Classroom Math Teacher

Whether there is a school-wide or district-wide Big Idea assessment program in place or not, an individual classroom teacher can also include Step Five of the balanced program by following these guidelines:

1. Decide with colleagues the number strand Big Idea for each grade level

2. Find or create a performance task that evaluates student understanding of the grade's Big Idea

3. Make a task-specific rubric or scoring guide to evaluate student performance and share it with students before they complete the task

4. Administer the performance task as a formative assessment to students early in the school year

5. Evaluate student papers using the rubric or scoring guide and share results with students

6. Revise instructional strategies, lessons, and activities as needed based on student results

7. Give one or more similar performance tasks throughout the year, always providing students with the scoring guide before they complete task

8. Administer summative performance task the last month of school and evaluate with scoring guide to show individual growth of understanding of the Big Idea

9. Have students self-reflect at the end of the year about their progress in learning the Big Idea

Sounds easy, right? No? Teachers well know that it always takes a lot of work to institute a new program or practice. But the positive results for students far outweigh the time and effort involved. Increased student improvement and mathematical confidence will become evident over time.

Big Idea Performance Task Examples

We have included in the following pages selected Big Idea performance tasks from the first, fourth, and sixth grades that were used in Carlsbad Unified School District, Carlsbad, California as examples for the primary, intermediate, and middle school levels, respectively. We have also included the corresponding rubrics for the first and sixth grade tasks. A fourth grade rubric can be created using these as a guide. Carlsbad began the program with only one year-end summative assessment task per grade level but in subsequent years added three formative tasks per grade level. The practice tasks (not included here) were written in the same format as the final performance task, in both English and Spanish, to provide students with more opportunities to practice their particular Big Idea problems throughout the school year.

Big Idea Mathematics Performance Task
First Grade
Addition

- **Task Description:** In this task, students will write addition equations with two or three addends (for example: $2 + 3 = 5$, $2 + 3 + 5 = 10$)

- **Materials:** Worksheet and a pencil.

- **Conditions of the Work:** Students will work alone. The task should take about 30 minutes, but students may work until they complete the task.

- **Teacher Directions:** Read the problem to the students. Remind the students that they need to write three number sentences.

- **Standard Being Assessed:** Combine groups of objects to a total of 20, and write the correct addition equation.

Big Idea Mathematics Performance Task
First Grade
Addition

Problem: Look at the pictures. Use the pictures to make up 3 addition number sentences.

Number sentences:

Five Easy Steps to a Balanced Math Program

Big Idea Mathematics Performance Task Rubric
First Grade

- **Evidence that a paper is advanced:**

  - Student writes 3 correct number sentences (including the sum).
  - One of the correct number sentences includes three addends.
  - Number sentences match the pictures.

- **Evidence that a paper is proficient:**

  - Student writes two or three correct number sentences (including the sum).
  - Number sentences match the pictures.

- **Evidence that a paper is progressing:**

  - Student writes one correct number sentence (including the sum).
  - Number sentence matches the pictures.
  - Students does not write a correct math sentence.

Big Idea Mathematics Performance Task
Fourth Grade
Division

- **Task Description:** Students will solve a problem using division or multiplication. They will use words and numbers to show their understanding of division and multiplication.

- **Materials:** Worksheet and a pencil.

- **Conditions of the Work:** Students will work alone. The task should take approximately 40 minutes, but students may work until they complete the task.

- **Teacher Directions:** Read the problem to the students as they follow along on their worksheet.

  Remind students that they need to explain their answer using words and numbers.

- **Standards Being Assessed:** Analyze and solve problems in order to determine the appropriate operations. Demonstrate the application of multiplication facts up to 12 x 12 in a variety of ways.

Big Idea Mathematics Performance Task
Fourth Grade
Division

Problem: Julian Apple Company has 24 apples to give away to 8 people. If each person gets the same amount, how many apples will each person get?

Directions: Prove your answer using multiplication and division. Include words and numbers in your explanation.

Answer:

Numbers:

Writing:

Big Idea Mathematics Performance Task
Sixth Grade
Dividing With Fractions

- **Task Description:** In the first part of this task, students will explain what it means to divide a whole number by a fraction. In the second part of the task, students will draw fraction circle in order to show what the problem looks lik and what the answer equals.

- **Materials:** Worksheet and a pencil (no calculator needed).

- **Conditions of the Work:** Students will work alone. The task should take approximately 30 minutes, but students may work until they complete the task.

- **Teacher Directions:** Read the problem to the students as they follow along on their worksheet. Remind the students that there are two parts to the problem, and that they need to write out an explanation in part one, draw pictures in part two, and put their final answer in the answer box.

- **Standards Being Assessed:** Add, subtract, multiply, and divide fractions.

  Use mathematical language and representations with appropriate accuracy, including numerical tables, equations, simple algebraic equations and formulas, charts, graphs, and diagrams.

Big Idea Mathematics Performance Task
Sixth Grade
Dividing With Fractions

Problem:

Part One:
Explain in complete sentences what this problem means:

$$6 \div \frac{1}{2}$$

Part Two:
Draw fraction circles to determine the answer to the above problem.
Label all parts.

Answer:

Big Idea Mathematics Performance Task Rubric
Sixth Grade
Dividing With Fractions

- **Evidence that a paper is advanced:**

  - Student correctly completes both parts of the task and has correct answer in the answer box, (12).

  - Written explanation clearly expresses the concept of dividing a whole number by a fraction (how many halves are inside of six wholes).

  - Drawing shows six whole circles each divided in half. There is some sort of notation that states that each section equals $\frac{1}{2}$.

- **Evidence that a paper is proficient:**

  - Student completes both parts of the task and has correct answer in the answer box.

  - Written explanation expresses the concept of dividing a whole number by a fraction.

  - Drawing shows six whole circles each divided in half.

- **Evidence that a paper is progressing:**

  - Student completes only one part of the task and has incorrect answer in the answer box.

  - Written explanation missing or does not relate to the task.

  - Missing or incorrect drawing.

Increasing Ownership by Active Involvement

Even though these examples reflect many hours of research, revision, and refinement, we encourage teachers and districts to use the sample grade level Big Idea Performance Tasks and Rubrics as guides for developing their own. There is greater ownership and investment when those involved in beginning such a program in their own schools or districts do so. Just as each student is unique, so is each school and district unique. We hope readers will design Big Idea Performance Tasks and rubrics that reflect their own particular school and district culture. For more guidance in creating performance tasks and rubrics, please contact us using the information on the "How to Reach Us" page at the end of this book.

**Step Five
Reader's Assignment**

First decide if the "Big Idea" performance task is most appropriate to your individual classroom, your grade level, your school, or your entire district. After making this determination, follow the corresponding "roadmap" in this chapter that best meets your current needs and instructional responsibilities.

Implementing the Program in the K-8 Classroom

PART TWO

Introduction

Each step of our balanced math program can be successfully implemented in any grade, kindergarten through eighth, even though the instructional content changes and the level of complexity increases as students move from one grade to the next. Chapters Six, Seven, and Eight suggest specific lesson plans and provide sample problems for the primary, intermediate, and middle school classrooms, respectively. Chapter Nine offers time management ideas and practical tips for getting started.

We recognize that readers may want to read only the classroom implementation chapter that is closest to their current teaching assignment. If, however, you have decided to read all three in order to see the continuity and consistency of the program from one grade span to the next, you may notice certain information repeated. This was done to provide clarity for those who decide to read only one.

Regardless of the grade level they teach, both elementary and middle school math teachers need an effective time management system built into their daily math program. This is where knowing what's important to focus on and having a structured timeframe to carry it out become essential.

The following schedule serves as a helpful guideline for doing just that. Please note that this is a suggested schedule only, based on a one-hour math period. Given the ever-changing instructional needs of the students, teachers may need more time one week to emphasize certain steps of the balanced math program and less time the next. It is important to allow for this flexibility while striving to include all five steps in a consistent manner throughout the school year. In the next three chapters, the suggested time allotments for each step of the program will be more specific to the grade being addressed.

Suggested Time Management Applicable to All Grades K-8

- **Math Review**—approximately 20 minutes, four days a week

- **Mental Math**—approximately five minutes, four days a week

- **Conceptual Unit Lesson or Activity**—approximately 35 minutes, four days a week

- **Assessment Day**—once a week, usually Friday, including:

    – Math Review Quiz and

    – Math Facts Quiz or

    – Assessment to gauge student progress in Conceptual Unit

- **Problem-of-the-Week**—assigned every other week on Monday and completed Friday (substituted for Conceptual Unit lesson or activity that week)

- **Math Facts**—incorporated into Math Review and assigned for homework four days a week during weeks when Math Facts Quiz is scheduled

- **"Big Idea" Performance Task**—assessed at end of school year (either district-wide or within an individual school, grade level, or classroom)

CHAPTER

6

Inside the Primary Classroom

In this chapter, we show the application of the balanced math program model in a third grade classroom, but the same format will work equally well in kindergarten, first, and second grades. The duration of each component is based on an hour and fifteen-minute math class.

The lesson plan provided begins week one of the new school year, but the balanced math program can certainly be started at any time. It provides the specific daily problems for Math Review, Mental Math, and the Math Review Quiz.

Third Grade Math Review

On Monday through Thursday, each math class begins with Math Review as explained in Chapter One. Using the Math Review Template to help students develop proficiency in place value, addition, subtraction, multiplication (the Big Idea Conceptual Unit), and measurement, the teacher writes these five problems on the board for the students to solve:

Monday

$600 + 40 + 3 =$

Place Value

337
+ 267

Addition

40
- 7

Subtraction

Illustrate
3 x 6

**Multiplication—
Conceptual Unit**

1 meter = ___ centimeters
1 foot = ___ inches
1 yard = ___ feet

Measurement

Commentary

Because it is the start of a new school year and a new conceptual unit (multiplication), many students may not yet be able to solve all five of the problems. The teacher has several options.

S/he can work through the problems with the class as a whole, invite those requiring assistance to meet in an area of the room and work with the teacher, or encourage students to work with a partner at their desks. Any of these methods can easily take longer than the ideal 15 to 20 minutes. Recognize this and simply allow yourself more time in the beginning of the year to train the students to successfully complete Math Review.

Or the teacher may choose to only assign three problems for the students to solve, even though s/he won't be able to address as many concepts daily. We recommend five problems once the class is accustomed to the process. Also, as students become familiar with Math Review, the time it takes will be much shorter.

The next step is to process Math Review using any of the methods or approaches presented in Chapter One. Usually the *teacher-directed* approach is best at the beginning of the year because it provides the opportunity to demonstrate procedural process and show students how to think through the computational steps of a problem. Later, as students become more adept, *student-directed* correction of the five problems is fun and engaging for the class. We use the other methods to vary the routine as the year proceeds.

Third Grade Mental Math

Our experience has been that children love doing mental math problems *so long as* we say the problem at a moderate to slow speed and repeat the problem for those who "lose the answer" somewhere in the string of numbers and mathematical operations. For students who have no trouble keeping up, we tell them to calculate again on the second recitation to confirm or change their answer. This seems to keep everyone engaged and happy.

The first day of Mental Math in third grade looks, or rather, *sounds* like this:

Monday

1. Start with 2 x 3 (6); multiply by 3 (18); add 2 (20); add the number of inches in two feet. Answer? (44)

2. Start with 6 + 6 (12); add six (18); add six again (24); add 10 (34); subtract 4 (30); subtract 7. Answer? (23)

3. Start with 7 + 7 (14); add 7 (21); subtract 6 (15) multiply by 1. Answer? (15)

4. Start with 4 + 4 (8); add 4 (12); add 4 (16); subtract 7 (9); add 9 (18); add 9 again. Answer? (27)

Commentary

Four problems may be more than the teacher has time to do. Often two are sufficient. Choose the number of problems that are appropriate for your class and available time. If these particular problems are too difficult for your current class, make up easier ones with fewer steps and then make them more challenging as the year progresses and your students' confidence and ability improve.

We instruct the children to write down their answer for each Mental Math string underneath the Math Review problems of the day as soon as they've determined the answer. We then ask student volunteers to announce their answer. The rest of the class confirms or denies the answer by a show of "thumbs up" if they agree, "thumbs down" if they disagree, "thumbs to the side" if they're not sure.

Another method is to let everyone say the answer in unison. To prove the answer (and also to help those students who gave up during the problem because they lost track or couldn't keep up), we then repeat the problem aloud—part by part—and have students say aloud each part's answer. This helps keep everyone engaged, shows how the answer was determined, and encourages those struggling to try the next problem.

The following pages contain the Math Review and Mental Math problems that the third grade teacher will have students complete on Tuesday, Wednesday, and Thursday in the same manner as described above.

Tuesday

Math Review:

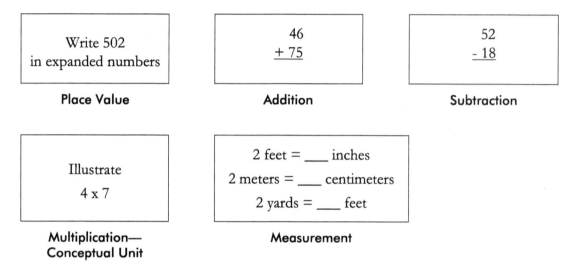

Write 502 in expanded numbers	46 + 75	52 - 18
Place Value	**Addition**	**Subtraction**

Illustrate
4 x 7

**Multiplication—
Conceptual Unit**

2 feet = ___ inches
2 meters = ___ centimeters
2 yards = ___ feet

Measurement

Mental Math:

1. Start with 6 x 2 (12); subtract 10 (2); subtract 2 (0); multiply by the number of feet in one yard. Answer? (0)

2. Start with 3 x 4 (12); multiply by 1 (12); add 2 (14); add the number of inches in one foot. Answer? (26)

3. Start with 2 + 5 (7); multiply by 2 (14); subtract 3 (11); subtract 2 (9); subtract 5 (4); multiply by 2. Answer? (8)

4. Start with 6 + 6 (12). Add 6 (18); subtract 6 (12); multiply by 1 (12).

Five Easy Steps to a Balanced Math Program

Wednesday

Math Review:

200 + 40 + 6 =	427 + 298	31 - 12
Place Value	**Addition**	**Subtraction**

Illustrate 3 x 5	24 inches = ___ feet 100 centimeters = ___ meters 3 feet = ___ yards
Multiplication— **Conceptual Unit**	**Measurement**

Mental Math:

1. Start with 20 − 3 (17). Subtract 7 (10); subtract 2 (8); multiply by 4 (32); add 3 (35); add the number of centimeters in one meter. Answer? (135)

2. Start with 14 − 4 (10). Subtract 5 (5); multiply by three (15); add 5 (20); subtract 5 (15); add the number of feet in one yard. Answer? (18)

3. Start with 7 − 3 (4). Add 10 (14). Multiply by 1 (14); subtract 7 (7); add 7 (14); subtract 10. Answer? (4)

4. Start with 3 + 3 (6). Add 3 (9); add 3 again (12); add 3 again (15); add 5 (20); add 5 again (25); add 5 again. Answer? (30)

Thursday

Math Review:

Write 847 in expanded form	$\begin{array}{r} 58 \\ + 76 \\ \hline \end{array}$	$\begin{array}{r} 60 \\ - 18 \\ \hline \end{array}$
Place Value	**Addition**	**Subtraction**

Show repeated addition for 5 x 4	3 feet = ____ inches ____ centimeters = 2 meters 6 yards = ____ feet
Multiplication— **Conceptual Unit**	**Measurement**

Mental Math:

1. Start with 30 − 8 (22); subtract 2 (20); subtract 3 (17); add 6 (23); add six again (29); multiply by 1. Answer? (29)

2. Start with 20 minus the number of inches in a foot (8). Multiply by 2 (16); subtract 8 (8); add 2 (10); add 10 (20); add ten again (30); add 10 again. Answer? (40)

3. Start with 25 + 5 (30); subtract 10 (20); add 5 (25); multiply by 2 (50).

4. Start with the number of eggs in a dozen minus the number of inches in a foot (0). Multiply by 3 (0); multiply by 4 (0); multiply by 5 (0).

Math Review Quiz

Friday is the day we give students the Math Review Quiz patterned after the problems they have practiced during Math Review that week. As described in Chapter One, the purpose of the Math Review Quiz is to assess students' current level of proficiency in math skills and concepts that they have studied up to this point in the school year.

The following Math Review Quiz of ten problems reflects the problems third graders practiced during the preceding week: two problems for each of the five kinds of problems.

Math Review Quiz—Week One:

1. | $600 + 30 + 6 =$

2. | Write 247 in expanded form

3. | $\begin{array}{r} 335 \\ + 278 \end{array}$

4. | $\begin{array}{r} 49 \\ + 27 \end{array}$

5. | $\begin{array}{r} 40 \\ - 18 \end{array}$

6. | $\begin{array}{r} 41 \\ - 22 \end{array}$

7. | Illustrate 4 x 3

8. | Show repeated addition for 6 x 3

9. | 1 foot = ___ inches
1 meter = ___ centimeters

10. | 2 feet = ___ inches
200 centimeters = ___ meters

Grading the Math Review Quiz

If appropriate, you may choose to have your students exchange papers and grade the quiz together as you read the answers and write them on the board or overhead projector. This enables students to receive immediate feedback on their performance. They will usually bring any problems to your attention as soon as they receive their quizzes back from classmates. You will of course need to make sure the papers have been scored accurately and assign an evaluative symbol to them, but this may expedite the grading process for you.

If having your students peer-grade one another's quizzes is unworkable for you, for whatever reasons (and we certainly understand this!), then simply collect the papers, score and record them yourself, and hand them back on Monday.

Math Review Self-Reflection

After in-class grading is finished, consider the wonderful practice of having your students turn their papers over to write a brief self-reflection paragraph that addresses their current Math Review Quiz performance and corresponding plan for improvement during the next week.

If you decide to grade the papers yourself, have students do the self-reflection activity after you return their papers the following Monday. This will help them focus on personal goals for improvement just as they're about to begin a new week of Math Review.

Daily Math Schedule

The time allotment for mathematics varies according to grade level and the number of instructional minutes mandated by the school district. As a general rule of thumb, however, elementary teachers devote about an hour to math five days a week. Because they are typically with the same students all day, that time can often be extended.

Third Grade Math Schedule

Continuing with our example, the third grade teacher striving to implement the first four steps of the balanced math program (Math Review & Mental Math, Conceptual Understanding, Problem Solving, and Mastery of Facts) decides to schedule math for an hour and 15 minutes daily. Since s/he wants the problem solving activities to reflect application of the current conceptual unit, s/he's not yet ready to assign a formal Problem-of-the-Week. That will commence in week three. Nor will the teacher begin the Mastery of Facts accountability program yet. S/he wants to explain this to parents at Back-to-School Night (or by means of a letter if the school year is already well underway) and introduce the program to students after that. This is how the teacher would roughly allocate math time each day:

Third Grade Math Schedule

Weeks One and Two

Monday through Thursday:

1. **Math Review** (10-15 minutes)

2. **Process Math Review** (5 minutes)

3. **Mental Math** (5 minutes)

4. **Conceptual Unit – Multiplication** (35 minutes)

5. **Assign Homework** – Conceptual Lesson extension, Computation skills practice, and/or extra Math Review practice for students who didn't pass Quiz— (10 minutes)

Total Minutes: 75 daily

Friday—Assessment Day:

1. **Math Review Quiz** (30 minutes)

2. **Grade Quiz together**—optional (10 minutes)

3. **Math Review Self-Reflection** – optional, but recommended (5 – 10 minutes)

4. **Assessment of Week's Conceptual Unit Learning** (30 minutes) OR

5. **Conceptual Lesson Game/Activity that Supports Unit** (30 minutes)

Total Minutes: 60 – 80

Week Three Schedule

We recommend introducing the Problem-of-the-Week during the third week of the school year or the third week after beginning the balanced math program in the classroom. This will (1) provide a full two weeks to establish the sequence of Math Review, Mental Math, and the Conceptual Unit with students and (2) provide students with two weeks of instruction geared to the Conceptual Unit. By then the students will be ready to apply their conceptual understanding to a problem-solving situation.

The following schedule incorporates the problem-solving activities discussed in Chapter Three. Notice the difference in the instructional sequence as compared with weeks one and two. The Problem-of-the-Week replaces the Conceptual Unit lesson, but it *applies that concept* in a problem-solving situation. The time allotments remain the same, with the Problem-of-the-Week activities given the same time as the Conceptual Unit activities.

Again, we strongly recommend completing the Problem-of-the-Week together as a class the first few times following the suggested daily sequence below. Students need to see the process modeled in class to thoroughly understand the day-by-day procedure of completing a Problem-of-the-Week Write-up. Once students are familiar with the process, they can work more independently and still follow the same schedule. Note: We assign for homework the completion of sections of the Problem-of-the-Week. If this is not workable in your particular situation, complete the entire process during the daily math class.

Monday:

1. **Math Review** (10-15 minutes)

2. **Process Math Review** (5 minutes)

3. **Mental Math** (5 minutes)

4. **Introduce Problem-of-the-Week** (35 minutes)

   - Explain problem thoroughly to class

   - Begin Data Sheet —using words, pictures, and numbers to solve problem

5. **Assign Homework** (10 minutes)

   - Finish attempting to solve Problem-of-the-Week on Data Sheet

   - Extra Math Review practice for students who didn't pass Math Review Quiz

Total Minutes: 70-75 daily during Problem Solving weeks

<u>**Tuesday:**</u> (Time allocations same as previous week)

1. **Math Review**

2. **Process Math Review**

3. **Mental Math**

4. **Data Sheet "Hint Day"**

    – Teacher checks to see students have worked on Data Sheet

    – Students who have solved problem give hints to students needing help

5. **Homework**

    – Revise and complete Data Sheet — due Wednesday

    – Extra Math Review practice for students who didn't pass Math Review Quiz

<u>**Wednesday:**</u> (Time allocations same)

1. **Math Review**

2. **Process Math Review**

3. **Mental Math**

4. **Problem-of-the-Week**

    – Correct answer now verified by teacher; students revise their Data Sheets to reflect correct answer and process

    – Data Sheets checked for completion according to directions

    – Teacher models Problem-of-the-Week Write-up using POW Guide

5. **Homework**

    – Students attempt first draft of Write-up

    – Extra Math Review Practice for students who didn't pass Math Review Quiz

Thursday: (Time allocations same)

1. **Math Review**

2. **Process Math Review**

3. **Mental Math**

4. **Problem-of-the-Week**

   – Continue modeling and revising together rough draft of Write-up using POW Guide

5. **Homework**

   – Write final draft of Problem-of-the-Week—due Friday

   – Extra Math Review practice for students who didn't pass Math Review Quiz

<u>**Friday:**</u>

1. Math Review Quiz (30 minutes)

2. Grade Quiz Together – optional (10 minutes)

3. Math Review Self-Reflection — optional, but recommended (5 – 10 minutes)

4. Process Problem-of-the Week (30 minutes)

   – Check for POW completion; students share Write-ups with class

   – Collect papers (evaluated only for completion and following directions)

   Total Minutes: 60 – 80

Week Four Schedule

In week four, the third grade teacher returns to the multiplication unit and continues to follow the same schedule as s/he did in weeks one and two. Depending on the length of the unit, s/he will try and include one or two more Problems-of-the-Week related to the unit focus in weeks five and seven (if the unit extends that long).

Evaluation of Progress

Throughout the grading period, the third graders receive weekly scores for their Math Review quizzes, feedback every two weeks or so for their progress in mastering multiplication facts (once the accountability program begins), and grades for weekly or biweekly chapter or unit assessments. At the culmination of the multiplication unit, the students complete a formal assessment (performance task) to demonstrate their full range of understanding of the math unit's focus statements or questions.

As described in Chapter Three, this performance task is self-assessed and teacher-assessed with a task-specific rubric. Once completed, students respond in writing to two or three self-reflection questions regarding their understanding of multiplication. They next place all their unit work, including the completed Problem-of-the-Week Write-ups, into a unit folder. The students then take their unit folders home for parent comments and return the folders to school for inclusion in their mathematics portfolio.

The third grade students and teacher now move on to the next unit, following the same procedure!

CHAPTER

7

Inside the
Intermediate Classroom

In this chapter, we show the application of the balanced math program model in a fifth grade classroom, but the same format will work equally well in fourth and sixth grades. Sixth grades that are part of the middle school should follow the format presented in Chapter Eight. The duration of each component is based on an hour and fifteen-minute math class.

The lesson plan provided here begins week one of the new school year, but the balanced math program can certainly be started at any time. It is identical in organization and pacing to the third grade lesson plan, but the daily problems for Math Review, Mental Math, and the Math Review Quiz are specific to fifth grade.

Fifth Grade Math Review

On Monday through Thursday, each math class begins with Math Review as explained in Chapter One. Using the Math Review Template to help students develop proficiency in place value, subtraction, multiplication and division, fractions (the Big Idea Conceptual Unit for fifth grade), and measurement, the teacher writes these five problems on the board for the students to solve.

Monday

Write 35,289 two ways	4010 - 1986	346 x 24
Place Value	**Subtraction**	**Multiplication/Division**

Illustrate $4\frac{3}{4}$	6 m = ___ cm ___ m = 5 km 5 ft = ___ in.
Conceptual Unit— **Fractions**	**Measurement**

Commentary

The teacher can work through the problems with the class as a whole, invite those requiring assistance to meet in an area of the room and work with the teacher, or encourage students to work with a partner at their desks. Any of these methods can easily take longer than the ideal of 10 to 15 minutes. Recognize this and simply allow more time in the beginning of the year to train the students to successfully complete Math Review. Once students become familiar with Math Review, the time it takes will be much shorter.

The next step is to process Math Review using any of the methods or approaches presented in Chapter One. Usually the *teacher-directed* approach is best at the beginning of the year because it affords the opportunity to demonstrate procedural process and show students how one thinks through the computational steps of a problem. Later, as students become more adept, *student-directed* correction of the five problems is fun and engaging for the class. Use the other methods to vary the routine as the year proceeds.

Fifth Grade Mental Math

Our experience has been that fifth graders, like third graders, love doing mental math problems *so long as* we say the problem at a moderate speed and repeat the problem for those students who "lose the answer" somewhere in the string of numbers and mathematical operations. For students who have no trouble keeping up, we tell them to calculate again on the second recitation to confirm or change their answer. This seems to keep everyone engaged.

The first day of Mental Math in fifth grade looks, or rather, *sounds* like the following. We have included the answers to each step, as well as the final answer, in parentheses:

Monday

1. Start with 3 x 5 (15); double that product (30); take ⅓ of that answer (10); multiply by 12 (120); take ¼ of that product. Answer? (30)

2. 6 x 7 + 3 (45); divide that answer by 9 (5); square that number (25); multiply by four (100); divide by 10 (10); subtract 10. Answer? (0)

3. 40 – 13 (27); divide by 3 (9); square that answer (81); add 9 (90); take ⅓ of that. Answer? (30)

4. 50 – 23 (27); add 3 (30); multiply by four (120); take ⅙ of that product (20); double that. Answer? (40)

Commentary

Four problems may be more than the teacher has time to do. Choose the number of problems that are appropriate for your class and available time. If these particular problems are too difficult for your current class, make up easier ones with fewer steps and then make the problems more challenging as the year progresses and students' confidence and ability improve.

We instruct the children to write down their answer for each Mental Math string underneath the Math Review problems of the day as soon as they've determined the answer. We then ask student volunteers to announce their answer. The rest of the class confirms or denies the answer by a show of "thumbs up" if they agree, "thumbs down" if they disagree, "thumbs to the side" if they're not sure.

Another method is to let everyone say the answer in unison. To prove the answer (and also to help those students who gave up during the problem because they lost track or couldn't keep up), we then repeat the problem aloud—part by part—and have students say aloud each part's answer. This helps keep everyone engaged, shows how the answer was determined, and encourages those struggling to try the next problem.

We strongly recommend that the teacher write down the given string of numbers and operations before reading each problem to the class. In our experience, we have tried to rely on memory, with less than favorable results!

The following pages contain the Math Review and Mental Math problems that the fifth grade teacher will have students complete on Tuesday, Wednesday, and Thursday in the same manner as described above.

Tuesday

Math Review:

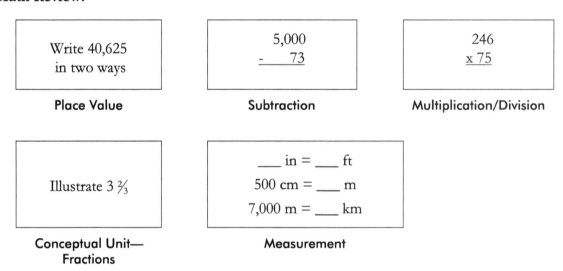

Write 40,625 in two ways	5,000 - 73	246 x 75
Place Value	**Subtraction**	**Multiplication/Division**

Illustrate 3 ⅔	___ in = ___ ft 500 cm = ___ m 7,000 m = ___ km
Conceptual Unit—Fractions	**Measurement**

Mental Math:

1. Start with the number of inches in two feet (24); double that answer (48); add two (50); multiply by three (150); divide by the number of feet in a yard (50); multiply by 10 . Answer? (500)

2. Start with the number of inches in a yard (36); add four (40); subtract number of inches in a foot (28); divide by 7 (4); square that number. Answer? (16)

3. Start with the number of centimeters in two meters (200); add number of meters in two kilometers (2200); add 300 (2500); divide by 5 (500); take half of that (250); take half again. Answer? (125)

4. 6 x 9 (54); add 6 (60); subtract 13 (47); add one (48); divide by number of inches in a foot. Answer? (4)

Wednesday

Math Review:

$$(95 \times 10{,}000) + (4 \times 1{,}000) + (5 \times 100) + (6 \times 1) =$$

Place Value

5,002 - 1891	5)342
Subtraction	**Multiplication/Division**

Illustrate 5 ⅞	___ inches = 5 feet ___ cm = 8 m ___ m = 6 km
Conceptual Unit— **Fractions**	**Measurement**

Mental Math:

1. 3 x 8 (24); divide by 6 (4); square that quotient (16); take ¼ of that. Answer? (4)

2. 7 x 9 (63); add 17 (80); divide that sum by two (40); take ¼ of that answer (10); take ½ of that answer (5); square that. Answer? (25)

3. 9 x 6 (54); take half of that product (27); divide by 9 (3); triple that quotient (9); square that answer (81); subtract number of inches in one yard. Answer? (45)

4 56 ÷ 8 (7); multiply that by 10 (70); take half of that (35); divide by 7 (5); add the number of centimeters in 5 meters. Answer? (505)

Thursday

Math Review:

$$(6 \times 10{,}000) + (3 \times 1{,}000) \times (8 \times 100) + (2 \times 1) =$$

Place Value

3,000
− 189

Subtraction

$8\overline{)798}$

Multiplication/Division

Illustrate $6\ {}^{3}/_{16}$

**Conceptual Unit—
Fractions**

120 inches = ___ ft

70 cm = ___ m

2,000 km = ___cm

Measurement

Mental Math:

1. 14 x 2 (28); subtract square root of 3 (19); multiply by 10 (190); add number of kilometers in 10,000 meters (200); divide by 10. Answer? (20)

2. 7 x 6 (42); subtract 16 (26); take half of that difference (13); divide that by two (6½); divide that again by two. Answer? (3¼).

3. 36 ÷ 6 (6); square that quotient (36); double that answer (72); add 18 (90); subtract 50 (40); divide that difference by the number of legs on a spider. Answer? (5)

4. 15 + 15 + 15 (45); divide by 9 (5); add the number of yards in 15 feet (8); triple that sum (24); subtract the number of eggs in half a dozen. Answer? (18)

Math Review Quiz

Friday is the day we give students the Math Review Quiz patterned after the problems they have practiced during Math Review that week. As described in Chapter One, the purpose of the Math Review Quiz is to assess students' current level of proficiency in math skills and concepts that they have studied up to this point in the school year.

The following Math Review Quiz of ten problems reflects the ones fifth graders practiced during the preceding week: two problems for each of the five kinds of problems.

Math Review Quiz—Week One:

1. Write 43,879 in two ways using expanded notation

Answers: (1) 40,000 + 3,000 + 800 + 700 + 7
(2) 4 x 10,000 + 3 x 1,000 + 8 x 100 + 7 x 10 + 9 x 1 (either with/without parentheses)

2. Write the number for (6 x 10,000) + (4 x 1,000) + (7 x 100) + (3 x 10) + (6 x 1) =

3.
$$5{,}000$$
$$-\ \ \ 187$$

4.
$$4023$$
$$-\ 1872$$

5.
$$346$$
$$\times\ 37$$

6.
$$6\overline{)537}$$

7. Illustrate $4\frac{3}{4}$

8.

Illustrate 2⅔

9.

48 inches = ___ ft   200 cm = ___ m   7,000 m = ___ km

10.

6 ft = ___ inches   6 m = ___ cm   5 km = ___ m

Grading the Math Review Quiz

If appropriate, you may choose to have your students exchange papers and grade the quiz together as you read the answers and write them on the board or overhead projector. This enables students to receive immediate feedback on their performance. They will usually bring any problems to your attention as soon as they receive their quizzes back from classmates. You will of course need to make sure the papers have been scored accurately and assign an evaluative symbol to them, but this may expedite the grading process for you.

If having your students peer-grade one another's quizzes is unworkable for you, for whatever reasons (and we certainly understand this!), then simply collect the papers, score and record them yourself, and hand them back on Monday.

Math Review Self-Reflection

After in-class grading is finished, consider having your students turn their papers over to write a brief self-reflection paragraph that addresses their current Math Review Quiz performance and corresponding plan for improvement during the next week.

If you decide to grade and return their papers the following Monday, have students do the self-reflection activity then. This will help them focus on personal goals for improvement just as they're about to begin a new week of Math Review.

Daily Math Schedule

The time allotment for mathematics varies according to grade level and the number of instructional minutes mandated by the school district. As a general rule of thumb, however, elementary teachers devote about an hour or more to math five days a week. Because they are typically with the same students all day, that time can often be extended, but in middle school where the school day is marked by six to eight periods (unless the school is on a block or modified block schedule), that time frame is shorter.

Fifth Grade Math Schedule

In the fifth grade classroom the teacher striving to implement the first steps of our balanced math program (Math Review & Mental Math, Conceptual Understanding, Problem Solving, and Mastery of Facts) decides to schedule math for 75 minutes daily.

Since s/he wants the problem solving activities to reflect application of the current Conceptual Unit of fractions, s/he's not yet ready to assign a formal Problem-of-the-Week. That will commence in week three. Nor will the teacher begin the Mastery of Facts accountability program yet. S/he wants to explain this to parents at Back-to-School Night (or by means of a letter if the school year is already well underway) and introduce the plan to students after that.

This is how the teacher roughly allocates math time each day:

Fifth Grade Math Schedule

Weeks One and Two

Monday through Thursday:

1. **Math Review** (15 minutes)

2. **Process Math Review** (10 minutes)

3. **Mental Math** (5 minutes)

4. **Conceptual Unit – Fractions** (35 minutes)

5. **Assign Homework** – Conceptual Lesson extension, Computation skills practice, and/or extra Math Review practice for students who didn't pass Quiz— (10 minutes)

Total Minutes: 75 daily

Friday—Assessment Day:

1. **Math Review Quiz** (30 minutes)

2. **Grade Quiz together**—optional (10 minutes)

3. **Math Review Self-Reflection** – optional, but recommended (5 – 10 minutes)

4. **Assessment of Week's Conceptual Unit Learning** (30 minutes) OR

5. **Conceptual Lesson Game/Activity that Supports Unit** (30 minutes)

Total Minutes: 60 – 80

Week Three Schedule

We recommend introducing the Problem-of-the-Week during the third week of the school year or the third week after beginning the balanced math program in the classroom. This will (1) provide a full two weeks to establish the sequence of Math Review, Mental Math, and the Conceptual Unit with students and (2) provide students with two weeks of instruction geared to the Conceptual Unit. By then the students will be ready to apply their conceptual understanding to a problem-solving situation.

The following schedule incorporates the problem-solving activities discussed in Chapter Three. Notice the difference in the instructional sequence as compared with weeks one and two. The Problem-of-the-Week replaces the Conceptual Unit lesson, but it *applies that concept* in a problem-solving situation. The time allotments remain the same, with the Problem-of-the-Week activities given the same time as the Conceptual Unit activities.

As we explained in Chapter Three, we strongly recommend completing the Problem-of-the-Week together as a class the first few times following the suggested daily sequence below. Students need to see the process modeled in class to thoroughly understand the day-by-day procedure of completing a Problem-of-the-Week write-up. Once students are familiar with the process, they can work more independently and still follow the same schedule. Note: We assign for homework the completion of sections of the Problem-of-the-Week. If this is not workable in your particular situation, complete the entire process during the daily math class.

Monday:

1. **Math Review** (10-15 minutes)

2. **Process Math Review** (5 minutes)

3. **Mental Math** (5 minutes)

4. **Introduce Problem-of-the-Week** (35 minutes)

   - Explain problem thoroughly to class

   - Begin Data Sheet —using words, pictures, and numbers to solve problem

5. **Assign Homework** (10 minutes)

   - Finish attempting to solve Problem-of-the-Week on Data Sheet

   - Extra Math Review practice for students who didn't pass Math Review Quiz

   - Extra Math Review Practice for students who didn't pass Quiz

Total Minutes: 70-75 daily during Problem Solving weeks

Tuesday: (Time allocations same as previous week)

1. **Math Review**

2. **Process Math Review**

3. **Mental Math**

4. **Data Sheet "Hint Day"**

   - Teacher checks to see students have worked on Data Sheet

   - Students who have solved problem give hints to students needing help

5. **Homework**

   - Revise and complete Data Sheet — due Wednesday

   - Extra Math Review practice for students who didn't pass Math Review Quiz

Wednesday: (Time allocations same)

1. **Math Review**

2. **Process Math Review**

3. **Mental Math**

4. **Problem-of-the-Week**

   - Correct answer now verified by teacher; students revise their Data Sheets to reflect correct answer and process

   - Data Sheets checked for completion according to directions

   - Teacher models Problem-of-the-Week Write-up using POW Guide

5. **Homework**

   - Students attempt first draft of Write-up

   - Extra Math Review Practice for students who didn't pass Math Review Quiz

Thursday: (Time allocations same)

1. **Math Review**

2. **Process Math Review**

3. **Mental Math**

4. **Problem-of-the-Week**

   – Continue modeling and revising together rough draft of Write-up using POW Guide

5. **Homework**

   – Write Final Draft of Problem-of-the-Week—due Friday

   – Extra Math Review Practice for students who didn't pass Quiz

Friday:

1. **Math Review Quiz** (30 minutes)

2. **Grade Quiz Together** – optional (10 minutes)

3. **Math Review Self-Reflection** — optional, but recommended (5 – 10 minutes)

4. **Process Problem-of-the Week** (30 minutes)

   – Check for POW completion; students share Write-ups with class

   – Collect papers (evaluated only for completion and following directions)

   Total Minutes: 60 – 80

Week Four Schedule

In week four, the fifth grade teacher returns to the Conceptual Unit in fractions and continues to follow the same schedule as s/he did in weeks one and two. Depending on the length of the unit, s/he will try to include one or two more Problems-of-the-Week related to the unit focus in weeks five and seven (if the unit extends that long).

Evaluation of Progress

Throughout the grading period, the fifth graders receive weekly scores for their Math Review quizzes, feedback every two weeks or so on their progress in mastering multiplication facts (once the accountability program begins), and grades for weekly or biweekly unit assessments. At the culmination of the fraction unit, the students complete a formal assessment (performance task) to demonstrate their full range of understanding of the fraction unit's focus statements or questions.

As described in Chapter Three, this performance task is self-assessed and teacher-assessed with a task-specific rubric. Once completed, students respond in writing to two or three self-reflection questions regarding their understanding of multiplication. They next place all their unit work, including the completed Problem-of-the-Week write-ups, into a unit folder. The students then take their unit folders home for parent comments and return the folders to school for inclusion in their mathematics portfolio.

As the third grade students did after completing the multiplication unit, the fifth grade students and teacher now move on to their next unit, following the same procedure!

CHAPTER

8

Inside the
Middle School Classroom

In this chapter, we show the application of the balanced math program in a middle school classroom with a 54-minute class period. Teachers in schools using a block schedule or modified block schedule will need to adjust their time allocations for each component according to their available number of daily or weekly minutes.

Seventh Grade Math Review

On Monday through Thursday, as in the primary and intermediate grades, each middle school math class begins with Math Review and Mental Math as explained in Chapter One. In middle school, however, the Math Review Quiz is given every *other* Friday, not weekly. The sample four-week lesson plan included in this chapter suggests specific daily problems for Math Review and Mental Math, as well as two Math Review Quizzes.

The Middle School Challenge

The challenge of middle school mathematics is to move students toward more complex mathematics (that is, algebra) while at the same time maintaining their basic math skills and their ability to determine a reasonable answer.

Math Review problems for middle school students need to reflect state standards, standardized test items, and the current unit of study. To successfully prepare students to understand algebra, Math Review problems continually need to reinforce skills related to fractions, decimals, and percents. To present isolated computational problems at the middle school level is not successful; the Math Review problems need to flow from and directly relate to the current Conceptual Unit and to the kinds of problems they will encounter on the state test.

Following are some ideas to consider when utilizing Math Review in the middle school classroom:

- Emphasize fractions, decimals, and percents: again, very important to success in algebra.

- Be persistent and maintain process enthusiastically. It pays off with this age group.

- Watch the time and try to keep it to about 15 minutes. It can easily take over your entire period if you're not careful.

- Assess every two weeks. Frequent assessment is very important for this age group. So much is happening in their lives, they constantly need to know how they are doing.

- Make sure numbers do not become cumbersome; keep computation reasonable to allow students to focus on concept. (Example: multiplying mixed numbers can become computationally cumbersome if you're not careful of the examples you create.)

As in the earlier grades, seventh grade math review can be fit into the Math Review Template, so that it is clear to students what types of problems they are practicing. The first day of Math Review might look like this:

Monday

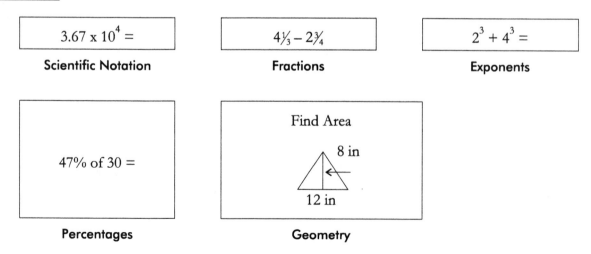

$3.67 \times 10^4 =$

Scientific Notation

$4\frac{1}{3} - 2\frac{3}{4}$

Fractions

$2^3 + 4^3 =$

Exponents

47% of $30 =$

Percentages

Find Area

8 in

12 in

Geometry

Commentary

When processing Math Review with students, be sure to emphasize (1) test-taking strategies, (2) the most common mistake made on a particular type of problem, and (3) reasonable answer. We offer here a few different suggestions for processing Math Review than those presented in Chapter One:

- **Row Expert.** The first student to finish in a student row (or cooperative team) begins to assist other students in that row with the day's assigned problems. During this time, the row expert discusses solutions with other students in that row who have also completed the problems. Such conversations prove invaluable for students who haven't yet mastered the concepts being presented.

- **Row Representative.** Assign each row (or team) of students a certain problem that they must solve and reach consensus on. After all students have completed the day's problems, the row (or cooperative team) representative shares with the class the group answer to their assigned problem and describes how they determined their answer.

- **Math Vocabulary.** Encourage students to use related math vocabulary and write related formulas and rules next to the problems as they are solved and later shared. (For example, students write rules that pertain to negative and positive integers).

- **Identify Math Concept.** Students identify key math concepts being practiced in given problems.

- **Common Mistake.** Teacher alerts students to most common mistake made on particular problem to help them avoid repeating it.

Seventh Grade Mental Math

Middle school students enjoy Mental Math so long as we say the problem at a moderate speed and repeat the problem for those students who "lose the answer" somewhere in the string of numbers and mathematical operations. For students who have no trouble keeping up, we tell them to calculate again on the second recitation to confirm or change their answer. This seems to keep everyone engaged.

The first day of Mental Math looks, or rather, *sounds* like the following. We have included the answers to each step, as well as the final answer, in parentheses:

Week One

Monday—Week One

1. Start with 4 squared (16); add 2 cubed (24); add one (25); take the square root of that. Answer? (5)

2. Start with 10 minus ¾ (9¼); subtract ¼ (9); take the square root of that (3); multiply by 12 (36); add 4 (40); take 25 percent of the sum. Answer? (10)

3. Student-prepared mental math problem

Commentary

In addition to the Chapter One suggestions for incorporating Mental Math into the daily math program, here are additional guidelines for creating Mental Math problems specific to the middle school classroom:

- Incorporate key math concepts being addressed in Math Review problems

- Include percents, fractions, and decimals

- Include typical number patterns middle school students need to know:
  – powers of 10
  – square numbers and square roots
  – Pythagorean triples
  – fraction – decimal equivalency

We advocate students creating their own Mental Math problems and solutions and coming to class prepared to present them to their peers. Due to time constraints, we do limit the number of problems for any given day to three. We strive to increase active participation by all students with effective motivational techniques (i.e. sharing answer with neighbor, everyone saying answer in unison, holding up paper with answer, etc.).

The following pages contain Math Review and Mental Math problems that the middle school teacher, as well as the Week Four Math Review Quiz, that the middle school teacher will have students complete during the rest of Week One and all of Weeks Two, Three, and Four in the same manner as described above. You'll notice that not every week has problems for each day. By referring to the Four-week Schedule later on in this chapter, you'll see that the reason for this is that the time constraints for certain activities (for example, the Friday Discussion) do not allow for the inclusion of all the activities that day.

Tuesday—Week One

Math Review:

$47 \times 10^3 =$

Scientific Notation

$6\frac{3}{7} - 9\frac{4}{9}$

Fractions

$\sqrt{81} + \sqrt{64}$

Square Roots

28% of $120 =$

Percentage

Find Area

8.5 in, 4.5 in

Geometry

Mental Math:

1. Start with the $\sqrt{144}$ (12); add the $\sqrt{81}$ (21); divide that by 7 (3); cube the result (27); add 3 (30); multiply by 4. Answer? (120)

2. Start with 12 minus ¼ (11¾); subtract ½ (11¼); subtract ¼ (11); subtract 1 (10); cube the result (1,000); take 50% of that. Answer? (500)

3. Student prepared mental math

Wednesday—Week One

Math Review:

$3.5 \times 10^3 =$	$17 - \frac{3}{7} =$	$2^3 + 4^3 + 5^2 =$
Scientific Notation	**Fractions**	**Exponents**

37% of $15 =$	Find Area 24cm
Percentage	**Geometry**

Mental Math:

1. Start with 5 cubed (125); add 2 cubed (129); add 1 (130) take 50% of that (65); subtract 5 (60); take 25% of that. Answer? (15)

2. Start with 14 minus 2/3 (13 1/3); subtract 1/3 (13); multiply by 3 (39); add 1 (40); divide by 10 (4); subtract 2 squared. Answer? (0)

3. Student prepared mental math

Thursday—Week One

Math Review:

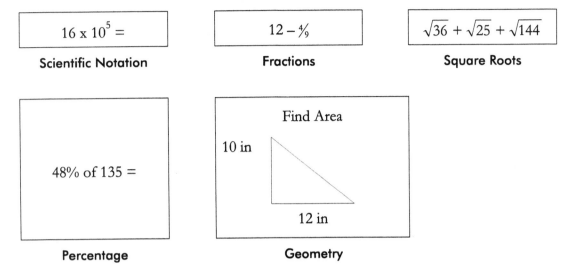

$16 \times 10^5 =$	$12 - \frac{4}{9}$	$\sqrt{36} + \sqrt{25} + \sqrt{144}$
Scientific Notation	**Fractions**	**Square Roots**

48% of 135 =

Percentage

Find Area

10 in

12 in

Geometry

Mental Math:

1. Start with 6 squared (36); add 3 squared (45); divide that by 5 (9); take the square root of the result. Answer? (3)

2. Start with 15 minus ½ (14 ½); subtract ½ (14); multiply by 2 (28); divide by 7 (4); cube the result (64); take 50% of that (32); take 25% of the result. Answer? (8)

3. Student prepared mental math

Friday—Week One

Math Review:

$6.7 \times 10^5 =$

Scientific Notation

$8\frac{1}{6} - 3\frac{4}{5} =$

Fractions

$9^2 + 3^3 + 6^2 =$

Exponents

65% of $50 =$

Percentage

Find Area

12cm

14cm

Geometry

Week Two

In the interest of saving space, we have opted simply to list the Math Review and Mental Math problems for your use from now on. Now that you are familiar with the Math Review Template and the "script" for mental math, you can translate the problems into these formats on your own.

Monday—Week Two

Math Review:

1. (Scientific Notation) $5.267 \times 10^5 =$

2. (Fractions) $8\frac{2}{3} + 9\frac{3}{5} =$

3. (Exponents) $2^3 + 3^2 + 4^3 =$

4. (Percentage) 27% of $65 =$

5. (Geometry) Find Area

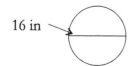
16 in

Five Easy Steps to a Balanced Math Program

Mental Math:

1. 5×10^{3} (5000) 50% of result (2500) take the square root of the result (50) $\frac{1}{5}$ of result (10)
   = 10

2. $5\frac{1}{2} + 3\frac{1}{2}$ (9) take the square root of the result (81) $+ \sqrt{25}$ (86) $+ \sqrt{16}$ (90) divide by 10
   (9) $- \frac{2}{5}$ ($8\frac{3}{5}$) $= 8\frac{3}{5}$

3. Student prepared mental math

Tuesday—Week Two

Math Review:

1. (Scientific Notation) $4 \times 10^{6} =$

2. (Fractions) $5\frac{1}{6} - 2\frac{2}{3} =$

3. (Square Roots) $\sqrt{144} + \sqrt{225} + \sqrt{1} =$

4. (Percentage) 100% of 5 =

5. (Geometry) Find Area

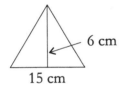

6 cm

15 cm

Mental Math:

1. Area of triangle with base of 10 and height of 4 (20) 50% of result (10) take the square root of the result (100) + 44 (144) take the square root of the result (12) = 12

2. 6×10^{2} (60) 25% of result (15) $+ \sqrt{64}$ (23) $- 7$ (16) $- \frac{4}{7}$ ($15\frac{3}{7}$) $= 15\frac{3}{7}$

3. Student prepared mental math

Thursday—Week Two

Math Review:

1. (Scientific Notation) $7.23 \times 10^{7} =$

2. (Fractions) $18 - \frac{4}{5} =$

3. (Square Roots) $\sqrt{81} + \sqrt{49} + \sqrt{100} =$

4. (Percentage) 12% of 12 =

5. (Geometry) Find Area

                                                 28.5 cm

            7.5 cm

Thursday—Week Two

Mental Math:

1. Area of triangle with base of 16 and height of 10 (80) 25% of result (20) 25% of result (5) + 2 ½ (7½) + ¾ (8¼) = 8¼

2. $\sqrt{49}$ (7) + $\sqrt{144}$ (19) + $\sqrt{1}$ (20) $\times 10^{3}$ (20,000) = 20,000

3. Student prepared mental math

Friday—Week Two

Math Review Quiz (see next section)

Week Three

Tuesday—Week Three

Math Review:

1. (Scientific Notation) write 250,000 using scientific notation

2. (Fractions) $3\frac{1}{4} \times 2\frac{4}{5} =$

3. (Fractions) $4\frac{1}{3} \div \frac{3}{5} =$

4. (Integers) $-6 - (-12) =$

5. (Geometry) Find x

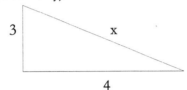

Mental Math:

1. 8 divided by $\frac{1}{4}$ (32) + -8 (24) + -4 (20) divide by $\frac{1}{5}$ (100) = 100

2. $-7 - 8$ (-15) $+7$ (-8) -9 (-17) $+ 25$ (8) = 8

3. Student prepared mental math

Wednesday—Week Three

Math Review:

1. (Scientific Notation) write 346,000,000 using scientific notation

2. (Fractions) $4\frac{1}{2} \times 3\frac{2}{3} =$

3. (Fractions) $9 \div \frac{3}{4} =$

4. (Integers) $(-2 \times -4)(-6) =$

5. (Geometry) Find x

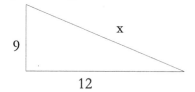

Mental Math:

1. 4 divided by ½ (8) + -16 (-8) take the square root of the result (64) + -4 (60) 25% of result (15) = 15

2. $-10 - 10$ (-20) + 4 (-16) - -10 (-6) = -6

3. Student prepared mental math

Thursday—Week Three

Math Review:

1. (Scientific Notation) write 750,000 using scientific notation

2. (Fractions) $6\frac{1}{3} \times 4\frac{1}{5} =$

3. (Fractions) $5\frac{1}{2} \div \frac{3}{4} =$

4. (Integers) $-6 -7 -8 +9 =$

5. (Geometry) Find

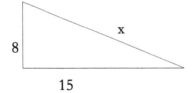

Mental Math:

1. 8 divided by $\frac{1}{3}$ (24) 50% of result (12) 25% of result (3) divide by $\frac{1}{12}$ (36) = 36

2. $8 - 12$ (-4) $+ -6$ (-10) $+ -9$ (-19) $- 7$ (-12) = -12

3. Student prepared mental math

Friday—Week Three

Math Review:

1. (Scientific Notation) write 2,650,000 using scientific notation

2. (Fractions) $2\frac{2}{5} \times 3\frac{1}{3} =$

3. (Fractions) $6 \div \frac{3}{5} =$

4. (Integers) $-8 +9 -7 -6 =$

5. (Geometry) Find x

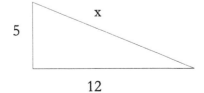

Week Four

Monday—Week Four

Math Review:

1. (Scientific Notation) $4.27 \times 10^3 =$

2. (Fractions) $2\frac{1}{2} \times 2\frac{1}{3} =$

3. (Fractions) $49 \div \frac{1}{7} =$

4. (Integers) $(-6)(-5) =$

5. (Geometry) Find x

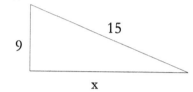

Mental Math:

1. Name missing part of each Pythagorean triple: 3,4,_____ (5)
   8,15,____ (17)   6,8,____ (10)   10,24,____ (26)

2. $2.67 \times 10^2 = (26.700)$
   $4.5 \times 10^3 = (4,500)$
   $2.8 \times 10^4 = (28,000)$

3. Student prepared mental math

Tuesday—Week Four

Math Review:

1. (Scientific Notation) $2.374 \times 10^5 =$

2. (Fractions) $4\frac{2}{3} \times 2\frac{1}{5} =$

3. (Fractions) $3\frac{2}{3} \div \frac{2}{5} =$

4. (Integers) $(9)(-5) =$

5. (Geometry) Find x

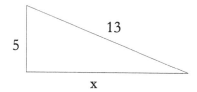

Mental Math:

1. Name missing part of triples: 3,__(4), 5   5,__(12), 13   8,__(15), 17

2. 8 divided by $\frac{1}{6}$ (48) + 2 (50) square the result (2500) = 2500

3. Student prepared mental math

Thursday—Week Four

Math Review:

1. (Scientific Notation) $6.378 \times 10^{6} =$

2. (Fractions) $3\frac{1}{2} \times 3\frac{2}{3}$

3. (Fractions) $3\frac{1}{5} \div \frac{1}{4} =$

4. (Integers) $5 -12 -7 +8 =$

5. (Geometry) Find x

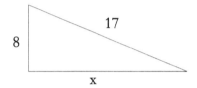

Mental Math:

1. -7×-8 (56) $+4$ (60) divide by -10 (-6) $+ 26$ (20) $= 20$

2. $-6 + 12$ (6) $- 9$ (-3) $- 12$ (-15) divide by 5 (-3) $= -3$

3. Student prepared mental math

Friday—Week Four

Math Review Quiz (see next section)

Seventh Grade Math Review Quiz

Whereas, in the primary and intermediate grades, the Math Review Quiz is administered on a weekly basis, we have found it more efficient only to have them every other week. They should still reflect the problems that the students have been practicing in Math Review for the two weeks leading up to each quiz.

Below are two quizzes, one for the end of the second week of the four week schedule and one for the fourth. There are two problems for each of the five kinds that students have been practicing.

Math Review Quiz—Week Two:

1. $3.67 \times 10^3 =$

2. $47 \times 10^3 =$

3. $4\frac{1}{3} - 2\frac{3}{4} =$

4. $5\frac{1}{6} + 3\frac{4}{7} =$

5. $8^2 + 7^3 =$

6. $\sqrt{9} + \sqrt{81} + \sqrt{49} =$

7. 15% of 25 =

8. 47% of 135 =

9. Find Area

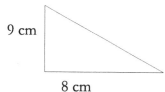

9 cm

8 cm

10.

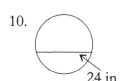

24 in

Math Review Quiz—Week Four:

1. $3.67 \times 10^4 =$

2. Write 254,000 using scientific notation

3. $2\frac{1}{3} \times 3\frac{1}{2} =$

4. $4\frac{1}{3} - 2\frac{3}{4} =$

5. $3\frac{1}{2} \div \frac{2}{3} =$

6. $16 \div \frac{1}{4} =$

7. $(-7)(2)(-3) =$

8. $5 - 6 - 7 + 8 - (-10) =$

9. Find x

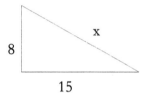

10. Find x

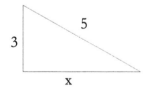

Grading the Math Review Quiz

Return the Friday Math Review Quiz to students the following Monday and review the quiz together as a class. In order to help students improve, we ask them to analyze their errors and write specific reasons why they missed a particular problem. Students then self-reflect on their overall performance and formulate a plan for improvement on the next quiz.

To help students see the connection between the Conceptual Unit and the Math Review Quiz, we add the quiz to the ongoing table of contents for the current Conceptual Unit.

Seventh Grade Conceptual Unit

The procedures for teaching a Conceptual Unit described in Chapter Two are very beneficial to middle school students, not only instructionally, but also from the standpoint of promoting good study habits and organizational skills. Setting objectives, keeping a running table of contents, and requiring a unit folder at the end of a Conceptual Unit helps middle school students know where teacher instruction is heading and heightens their sense of personal responsibility and accountability—especially when they must manage the instructional requirements and assignments from several teachers at once.

For the middle school teacher, establishing common instructional focus and Conceptual Unit objectives through discussions with departmental colleagues results in effective and consistent instruction and assessment methods for all students.

Seventh Grade Problem-of-the-Week

The middle school can follow the same basic schedule for problem solving as the elementary grades. Assigning a Problem-of-the-Week every other week (twice a month) is sufficient, especially given the time constraints of a 54-minute math period. There is one difference, however. At middle school, we assign the Data Sheet on Tuesday and require its completion by Friday. Only those students who bring a completed Data Sheet to class can participate in the Friday discussion about the problem. Those without Data Sheets work on a different assignment in another part of the room.

The Friday Discussion

The purpose of the Friday discussion is to enable students to share their ideas about the Problem-of-the-Week and the different techniques they have used to solve it. They also discuss ways that they can improve their data sheet. Those participating in the Friday discussion decide, based on their work and the ideas that are discussed, what they *think* is the correct answer. During the Friday discussion the teacher does not reveal the answer. Students must take from the discussion any additional insights to determine the actual answer and then finalize their own Data Sheet and Write-up.

The Write-up is due the following Tuesday, and students know that the "Work Section" must match the process followed on their Data Sheet. On Wednesday the correct answer is announced and discussed. This is immediately followed by peer-assessment and self-assessment of student papers using the Middle School POW Rubric.

Assessment Process

We have found that partner grading is not as effective at the middle school level due to student's intense interest in each other more than in the task at hand! It has proven more productive to use double scoring of student papers instead of partner scoring. One student assesses another student's paper. The paper is then assessed by a different student. Papers are returned to owners for self-assessment and then collected for the final grade determination by the teacher.

Mastery of Facts Commentary

In a middle school setting, number facts are reinforced during Math Review and Mental Math activities. Because of time constraints, a formal math fact program is not typical of the secondary math program. For this reason, middle school math teachers very much support the mastery of math facts accountability program at the elementary school level.

Daily Math Schedule

Since the time allotment for a middle school teacher is a fixed amount of time, a conceptual unit may take longer to get through than it would in elementary school. For this reason, we have provided a daily math schedule that extends over a four-week period, rather than a three-week period. This way the teacher can fit all components of the five steps without sacrificing student learning. This particular schedule is based on a 54-minute period, but you can adjust it to meet the specific needs of your schedule.

Seventh Grade Math Schedule

Week 1

Monday:

Math Review (15 minutes)

Mental Math (5 minutes)

Unit Lesson (34 minutes)

Tuesday:

Math Review (15 minutes)

Mental Math (5 minutes)

Unit Lesson (34 minutes)

Problem-of-the-Week assigned (data sheet due on Friday)

Wednesday:

Math Review (15 minutes)

Mental Math (5 minutes)

Unit Lesson (34 minutes)

Thursday:

Math Review (15 minutes)

Mental Math (5 minutes)

Unit Lesson (34 minutes)

Friday:

Math Review (15 minutes)

Data sheet discussion (35 minutes)

Week 2

Monday:

Math Review (15 minutes)

Mental Math (5 minutes)

Unit Lesson (34 minutes)

Tuesday:

Math Review (15 minutes)

Mental Math (5 minutes)

Unit Lesson (34 minutes)

Problem-of-the-Week Write-up due

Wednesday:

Process/peer assess problem (wait one day to process to allow for late papers) (54 minutes)

Thursday:

Math Review (15 minutes)

Mental Math (5 minutes)

Unit Lesson (34 minutes)

Friday:

Math Review Quiz/Grade quiz in class together (50 minutes)

Week 3

Monday:

Process Math Review quiz/error analysis and self reflection (30 minutes)

Unit Lesson (34 minutes)

Tuesday:

Math Review (15 minutes)

Mental Math (5 minutes)

Unit Lesson (34 minutes)

Assign Problem-of-the-Week (data sheet due Friday)

Wednesday:

Math Review (15 minutes)

Mental Math (5 minutes)

Unit Lesson (34 minutes)

Thursday:

Math Review (15 minutes)

Mental Math (5 minutes)

Unit Lesson (34 minutes)

Friday:

Math Review (15 minutes)

Data sheet discussion (35 minutes)

Week 4

Monday:

Math Review (15 minutes)

Mental Math (5 minutes)

Unit Lesson (34 minutes)

Tuesday:

Math Review (15 minutes)

Mental Math (5 minutes)

Unit Lesson (34 minutes)

Problem-of-the-Week Write-up due

Wednesday:

Process/peer assess problem (54 minutes)

Thursday:

Math Review (15 minutes)

Mental Math (5 minutes)

Unit Lesson (34 minutes)

Friday:

Math Review quiz/grade together in class (50 minutes)

CHAPTER

9

Putting It All Together: Time Management & Practical Tips for Getting Started

So there you have it: the five steps to implementing a balanced math program! These steps do become easy once teachers understand the components of the program and begin applying them in their own classrooms. We hope the sample problems and lesson plans in the grade-specific classroom implementation chapters will assist you in creating your own Math Review and Mental Math problems and in scheduling your math time to include each of the five steps.

A Word About Time

Regardless of whether they teach first grade self-contained or eighth grade departmentalized, classroom teachers face the uncompromising constraints of the ever-ticking clock. An elementary teacher is responsible for teaching all of the academic content areas and must continually adjust the daily schedule to meet the demands of each. A middle school math teacher may only have one content area to teach but must work to create a balanced math program that addresses the needs of all students within a fixed time frame of 54 minutes or less. Recognizing the need for more time is one of the reasons why so many middle schools are moving to a block or modified block schedule. Hopefully you are concluding this book with new ideas for maximizing your instructional time and determining a workable framework for doing so.

Practical Tips for Getting Started

In the first five chapters, we have included the critical information and pertinent examples needed to enable any teacher to successfully implement each of the balanced math program steps. Here, we offer a summary of key ideas to help you begin:

1. Familiarize yourself with state, district, and grade level math standards and grade level learning expectations.

2. Collaborate with teachers above and below your own grade level to help build a systematic progression of math concepts from one grade to the next (curriculum mapping).

3. Decide the major units you plan to teach during the school year in consideration of state and district standards as well as concepts and skills students will encounter on the standardized test.

4. Determine the focus statements or questions for each of these Conceptual Units as you prepare to teach them.

5. Select formative and end-of-unit summative assessments (performance tasks) matched to the unit focus statements that afford students the opportunity to show all of their learning relative to the Conceptual Unit focus.

6. Plan your unit's lesson plans around the focus statements, utilizing the instructional materials, lessons, and activities that best advance student understanding of the unit focus.

7. Search out supplemental resources to use for Math Review, Mental Math, and your Problems-of-the Week.

8. Develop your grade-level Math Review Template.

9. Locate, borrow, purchase, or create your grade level Math Facts program.

10. Prepare your letter to inform parents of the math facts accountability program you intend to implement.

11. Write two or three Self-Reflection questions that students can respond to at the end of each math unit.

12. Review the Blackline masters in the appendix section of this book and decide which ones will be of use to you.

Your Work Will Pay Off!

We fully recognize the amount of initial thinking and preparation needed to implement a balanced math program *because we have done this work ourselves*! The first time you design a Conceptual Unit may be challenging. The first time you begin a Problem-of-the-Week with your students may seem daunting. The first time you write a math rubric with your students may be as much of an education for you as for your students. But once you've made each of these practices "your own," you will be able to continuously refine the process again and again, year after year. In providing your students with the necessary ingredients to become mathematically powerful, we think you'll agree that it was more than worth the effort.

If you have any questions, please don't hesitate to contact us. Our phone, fax, and e-mail information can be found on the "How to Reach Us" page at the end of this book. We will be more than happy to assist you in any way we can.

Good luck! Have fun! Be balanced!

References

Ainsworth, L. & Christinson, J. (1998). *Student Generated Rubrics: An Assessment Model to Help All Students Succeed.* Orangeburg, NY: Dale Seymour Publications.

Burns, M. (1999). *Math Solutions Newsletter.* Number 25, Spring/Summer 1999. (p. 4). Sausalito, CA: Marilyn Burns Education Associates.

Jakwerth, P. (1996, December). Curriculum and Achievement: Searching for the Empirical Link. *US National Research Center Report #7,* 12. (Third International Mathematics and Science Study, Michigan State University).

K-2 Performance Assessment Team. *K-7 Math Performance Task Binder.* San Diego County Office of Education, San Diego, CA.

Wiggins, G. & McTighe, J. (1998). *Understanding by Design.* Alexandria, VA: Association for Supervision and Curriculum Development.

Appendix

Blackline Masters

The blank forms in the pages that follow are included to give you a framework for planning a mathematics conceptual unit. Simply fill in the blanks.

Of course, it may help you to refer back to the corresponding chapters, and the classroom implementation chapter which corresponds to the grade level you teach. Once you have filled out all of these forms, the result should be a ready-to-teach conceptual unit that incorporates all of the five easy steps.

 The last form is a "Rubric for the Rubric," which you might consider giving to your grade-level associates or other colleagues to complete. This will help you develop more effective scoring guides in the future.

Should you need other examples or forms from the book and can't remember exactly where to find them, refer to the "List of Useful Forms and Examples" at the front of the book, behind the Table of Contents.

What *questions* do students have about _____?

1. _____

2. _____

3. _____

4. _____

5. _____

6. _____

7. _____

8. _____

What *essential understandings* do students need according to state/district/grade-level or subject matter content standards?

1. _____

2. _____

3. _____

4. _____

5. _____

6. _____

7. _____

8. _____

What *focus questions* could best combine what the students want to know and what I need to teach?

1. _____

2. _____

3. _____

4. _____

5. _____

6. _____

7. _____

8. _____

What will the *actual* focus qustions be?

1. _____

2. _____

3. _____

4. _____

What kind of *performance task* will best allow students to demonstrate their full understanding of the focus questions?

_____

_____

_____

_____

_____

What quizzes, tests, assessments will be needed to prepare them to successfully complete the performance task?

1. _____

2. _____

3. _____

4. _____

5. _____

6. _____

7. _____

8. _____

9. _____

What criteria do I want the *Rubric* to address?

1. _____
2. _____
3. _____
4. _____
5. _____
6. _____
7. _____
8. _____

What *self-reflection* questions do I want students to respond to at the conclusion of this unit?

1. _____
2. _____
3. _____
4. _____

What *lessons and activities* **do students need to understand the focus questions?**

_____

_____

_____

_____

_____

_____

_____

_____

_____

_____

_____

_____

_____

_____

_____

_____

_____

"A RUBRIC FOR THE RUBRIC"
Suggested Questions for
Providing Scoring Guide Feedback

Title of Rubric _____

Subject and Grade Level _____

Rubric Authors _____

Rubric Evaluators_____

1. Scoring guide is consistent with task requirements?

2. Scoring guide provides specific requirements for scores of exemplary, proficient, progressing, not yet meeting requirements?

3. Scoring guide written in "student language" with expectations for each level of performance easily understood?

4. Comments and suggestions for revision:

How to Reach Us

Jan Christinson

1769 Ave Vista Labera
Oceanside, CA 92056
Phone: (760) 945-0977
Email: jchristinson@makingstandardswork.com

Larry Ainsworth

Center for Performance Assessment
317 Inverness Way South, Suite 150
Englewood, CO 80112
Phone: (800) 844-6599
Email: Lainsworth@makingstandardswork.com

Five Easy Steps to a Balanced Math Program is also presented as a workshop for classroom teachers. Additional professional development workshops available through the Center for Performance Assessment include:

- Designing and Developing Standards-Based Performance Assessments

- Effective Teaching Strategies for the Standards-Based Classroom

- Advanced Seminar in Standards-Based Assessment

- Data-driven Decision Making

- Accountability in Action

For more information about the workshop on *Five Easy Steps to A Balanced Math Program* and other professional development opportunities, contact the Center for Performance Assessment at (800) 844-6599 or visit our web site at www.makingstandardswork.com.

Other Books by the Authors

By **Jan Christinson** and **Larry Ainsworth**:
Student Generated Rubrics: An Assessment Model to Help All Students Succeed
(Dale Seymour Publications)

By **Jan Christinson**:
Calculators and Mathematics Project, Los Angeles
(Cal State Fullerton Press)